Pastor Troy Evans is a pioneer and innovative leader in reaching and changing the lives of those who are trapped by the ways of the street with a relevant message of the cross of Christ wired to the hip-hop culture. This book is a long-awaited voice for the voiceless that will reveal the hope that is needed. It is not just for those serving in the city or those with gang backgrounds, but for those who serve anywhere broken people live. This book is for all ages, ethnicities, and genders because it is for those whose care comes from a place of pain.

—**Phil Jackson**, coauthor of *The Hip-Hop Church*,
lead pastor of The House Covenant Church

This book reflects its author; it's passionate and real. Through this book, Troy will compel you to reach people who are far from God in your context. Read and be inspired.

—**Chris Conrad**, district superintendent,
West Michigan District, The Wesleyan Church

Troy is one of my heroes! His life is a story of hope for countless youth trying to overcome the gang lifestyle. You too will be inspired by the story that God is writing in and through his life. This book is a must-read for anyone who wants to do ministry in the urban context.

—**Larry Acosta**, CEO, Urban Youth Workers Institute

For those called to reach this generation of urban America, this book will give you the tools you need to understand the culture. God has not forgotten our cities. He is only waiting for those who care about youth, to be better equipped to handle the business at hand.

—**Rod Thomas**, features producer, *The 700 Club*

The Edge of Redemption encompasses the best practices in youth development, cultural relevance to urban culture, and God's Word to provide a practical, research-based, how-to guide that inspires and prepares those serious about outreach to urban families.

—**Stacy Stout**, education director, Hispanic Center of Western Michigan

This book is a must-read; the story not only tells how God has taken a man from the edge of darkness and destruction into the center of his marvelous light, but it sheds light on the reality that so many young men and women are facing in cities across America today. It is ministries like The EDGE and ministers like Troy Evans God has raised up for such a time as this.

—**Dave Bever, Jr.**, lead pastor, New City Church, Cleveland, Ohio

The Edge of Redemption will help you understand today's youth as it gives you extremely practical suggestions on how individuals and churches can make room in their congregations for this new generation. This book is not only about how to work with the hip-hop generation, but is also about how God can redeem the brokenness of today's youth.

—**Henry Bouma**, executive director, R-House Ministries, Grand Rapids, Michigan

Troy does an incredible job of sharing his powerful story and weaving in application points throughout the book for the reader. The new multi-ethnic urban church is emerging everywhere, and we need more great resources like this!

—**Tommy "Urban D." Kyllonen**, Crossover Church, Tampa, Florida

THE **EDGE**
OF REDEMPTION

THE **EDGE**
OF REDEMPTION

A STORY OF HOPE FOR RESCUING THE UNREACHABLE

TROY A. EVANS

with Ann Byle

wesleyan
publishing
house

Indianapolis, Indiana

Copyright © 2011 by Troy Evans
Published by Wesleyan Publishing House
Indianapolis, Indiana 46250
Printed in the United States of America
ISBN: 978-0-89827-489-9

Library of Congress Cataloging-in-Publication Data

Evans, Troy D.
   The edge of redemption : a story of hope for rescuing the unreachable / Troy Evans with
Ann Byle.
       p. cm.
   ISBN 978-0-89827-489-9
1. Evans, Troy D. 2. Christian converts--Michigan--Grand Rapids--Biography.
3. Conversion--Christianity--Biography. 4. Church work with juvenile delinquents--
Michigan--Grand Rapids.   I. Byle, Ann E. II. Title.
   BV4935.E93A3 2011
   259'.5092--dc23
   [B]
                                                                    2011023903

Published in association with the literary agency of Credo Communications, LLC, Grand
Rapids, Michigan; www.credocommunications.net.

In memory of the late Dr. MaLinda Sapp and Geralden Bentley (Snooter, aka Gent), a seventeen-year-old young man I loved dearly and called my nephew, who was shot down and robbed in the inner city of Grand Rapids, Michigan. His brutal, unsolved murder became my breaking point; his death pushed me to say that the church must do something to reach the rough guys like I once was.

CONTENTS

Acknowledgments		11
Foreword		13

PART 1. THE LOST

1.	Lost Children	19
2.	Dreams in the Darkness	27
3.	Desecration	35
4.	Prey to Predator	43
5.	Blood Is Thicker	53

PART 2. THE PRODIGAL

6.	Filling the Void	63
7.	Street Wise	71
8.	The Gang Way	81
9.	Gang Family Values	91
10.	Respect of the Fallen	101
11.	Crossfire	111

PART 3. THE JOURNEY

12.	The Great Escape	121
13.	That Next Horizon	131
14.	Total Loss	139
15.	Into Salvation	147

PART 4. THE CHURCH

16. Transformed to Serve   159

17. Continuing Struggle   167

18. Approaching the Edge   179

19. The Church Applied   189

20. Afterword   199

Discussion Questions   211

ACKNOWLEDGMENTS

I am grateful to God for caring enough to send his Son to free me from the bondage of sin and destruction. I do not deserve the grace that has been extended to me through the blood of Jesus Christ. I also thank the Lord for my beautiful wife and best friend, LaDawn, who has loved me through all of my imperfections. You have shown me, by example, how to love. I cannot imagine life without you.

To my supportive children, Erin, Toni, Adrienne, and Anthony: Thank you for your willingness to share me with the rest of the world as I travel and minister to the lost. To my mom, Linda Love, my greatest supporter in the world: I thank you for always being there for me and believing in me.

To my dad, Gaylord Love: You are, and have always been, my Superman. Thank you for accepting and loving me as your boy when you did not have to. To all my siblings: I love you all for being patient with me even when I did not love myself. To my extended EDGE family: I love you with all of my heart and thank you for serving alongside me. I am so grateful for all of your love and support. I thank you, Denny Johnson, for helping me flesh out my thoughts and for encouraging me when I need it. Thank you to Pastor Wayne Schmidt, Pastor Kyle Ray, Henry Bouma, Mark Doane, Pastor Harold Stancle, Pastor Jermone Glenn, and Pastor Dave Beelen for always being willing to listen and believe in what God has entrusted me to do.

I also thank Larry Acosta, Phil Jackson, and Pastor Tommy "Urban D" for investing in me and always being a listening ear. I thank Andrew Wallace, Pastor Ronald Griffin, Kashawn Akins, and Pastor Rob Bush for showing me what it means to be a man of God. To my aunts, uncles, and cousins, I thank you for all of your support and for being real with me and loving me through my rough times. I especially thank those who endorsed this book and those I have interviewed in putting it together. A special thanks to Ann Byle for all of her hard work on this project.

I also want to thank Craig Q., B-Mack, and John for the many experiences we shared as youths and for your willingness to allow me to share some of them in this book. I also thank the whole McKinney family for taking me in as a young man and loving me as your own.

FOREWORD

It has been my privilege to connect with many wonderful ministry colleagues over the past three decades. Among them are a few who have been gifted by God in rare ways and experienced such an unusual life journey that they have a unique kingdom contribution to make. Such a man of God is Troy Evans.

I first met Troy, his wife LaDawn, and their family when they visited Kentwood Community Church (KCC), where I served as senior pastor. At the time, we were on our way to becoming a multiethnic church with an increasing desire to reach our community, a first-ring suburb of Grand Rapids, Michigan, where our local school hosted students from homes within which fifty-eight different languages are spoken. It was wonderful to welcome this African-American family, who combined spiritual depth with a heart for ministry to our community. They began serving with Kyle Ray, our outreach pastor, to help us impact the changing community immediately surrounding the church.

Some weeks later, I attended a conference that was conceived and promoted by Troy. The event focused on the reality of gangs in midsized cities like Grand

Rapids. It was obvious that Troy possessed what I call "convening" power—the capacity to bring together people who don't tend to, but need to, come together for the good of a community. That conference was attended by church leaders, law enforcement officers, community dignitaries, and gang leaders and members. A whole new world was opened up to me and many of those who attended. It was also a joy to see Troy's whole family engaged in hosting the event; it was obvious that some of his greatest joy came from doing ministry as family.

He also had the capacity to gain an audience with current gang leaders and knew the lay of the city. His background in music, dance, visual arts, and business prepared him to create a ministry that could reach people others could not. He helped create a hip-hop outreach named The EDGE Urban Fellowship.

I would learn from Troy that a vital ministry in an urban context had to be driven by so much more than a worship service. It took a variety of activities operating seven days a week to create enough connecting points with the various ages and life stages of those the ministry was called to reach. Being a hip-hop ministry, I expected the audience to be almost exclusively young and African-American. But those gathered were wonderfully diverse ethnically and generationally. The diversity of the crowd is a manifestation of Troy's vision to create a multiethnic ministry led by a multiethnic core team. (I also learned that my assumption that the consumers of rap music were only young African-Americans was a stereotype, and the music and culture attracted a far wider audience.)

Troy is a man who loves Jesus and his family and pays the price to reach a particular people group found in urban areas across America and around the world. The personal brokenness he experienced in his early years has been marvelously redeemed and recreated into a wholeness that makes it possible for him to live out the life of Jesus in the most challenging of neighborhoods.

Troy is passionate about reaching out and helping others. But his ministry has depth, too; people under his leadership become people of the Word and grow to love God completely and others unconditionally. He is a modern-day apostle Paul, reaching those others consider unreachable and paying the price that they might know abundant life, even in the face of suffering.

In my estimation, Troy has an apostolic gift, the God-given capacity not only to bring one ministry into existence, but also to catalyze a ministry multiplication movement. This is fueled by his commitment to multiplication of disciples and leaders. I believe he will influence the broader ministry community to become increasingly urban and multiethnic, a potential that will only be fully realized if others learn from him and join with him.

This book provides such a learning opportunity. May God use Troy's story and insights, as God has used Troy in my life, to broaden your view of ministry possibilities and inspire you to engage more fully in creative, fruitful kingdom work.

—Wayne Schmidt
Vice President for Wesley Seminary
at Indiana Wesleyan University

PART 1

THE LOST

1

LOST CHILDREN

From the earliest age, we are pushed to the edge.

Every book needs a little back story. I—and you—need to know where I came from to know where I'm going. Every day I look back on my journey and thank God for how he led me from darkness to light, from violence to peace, from ruthless to redeemed. My hope is that as God blessed me, he may bless you.

I am the third child and second son of my mother, Linda Evans Love. My sister Lisa, five years older than me, is the daughter of my mother's youth, born in 1966 when my mom was just seventeen. She was married to Lisa's father, Michael Evans; but he died in 1969 while in the U.S. Army. My brother Mark and I, fourteen months apart, are the birth sons of Mark Morgan, the pastor's son at the church we attended just a few minutes' walk from home. My parents' families had grown up together in the neighborhood, attending Davis Memorial Church of God in Christ (named in honor of my birth father's grandfather). My parents' relationship was short, but long enough to produce us boys.

I was born on August 21, 1972—a sultry day after what my mom describes as a long, hot summer. She laughs when she says she spent most of that summer sitting in front of a fan. I was born during the day at Butterworth Hospital in Grand Rapids after what my mom says was an easy labor. She had an apartment across the street from my grandma's place when Lisa, Mark, and I were each born.

Mark and I never had a relationship with our biological father. We attended the church our grandfather pastored, Davis Memorial, but never had much of a relationship with him, either. We called him Elder Morgan when we occasionally spoke to him. I've seen my father maybe six times in my life because he moved around a lot, and he didn't support us in any way. My mom cared for us alone until she met Gaylord Love when I was just six weeks old.

HOME AND FAMILY

Gaylord Love, the man I knew as my dad, met my mom in October 1972. Gaylord became the father figure in my life and the love of my mother's. He was a man's man—not very emotional or talkative, but he loved us and did things, especially sports, with us. We enjoyed weight lifting together, though I wasn't as much of an athlete as my brother Mark. Dad took us to the park, played a little catch, and taught us to ride bikes and fish. Together my mom and dad had two more children: my sister Teressa in 1981, and my brother Raymond in 1985. Gaylord and my mother both worked a couple of jobs each to feed us, clothe us, and keep us living in a decent house.

When we were young, my mom worked for the Grand Rapids Parks and Recreation Department as an activities coordinator at the Paul I. Phillips Gymnasium on the near southeast side of town. When we kids got older, she worked full time washing dishes at the Amway Grand Plaza Hotel during the week, and part time for the Parks and Recreation Department on the weekend. The Amway Grand was a long way from our neighborhood, not so much in distance but in status. The fancy hotel served the upper crust of

Grand Rapids and its guests. While they sipped champagne at the restaurants in the hotel or danced at a fundraising dinner, my mother ran the dishwashing machine. She eventually became assistant manager of the stewarding department, working there thirteen years. I worked there for a short time as well, before my mom had to fire me for coming in late to my shift.

My dad also worked two jobs. His full-time job as a security officer for Grand Rapids Public Schools took him away from home all week, and his weekends were usually filled with more work for the Parks and Recreation Department. Often he'd fall asleep—head lolling back, snoring, with his dinner plate tipping precariously in his lap—as he watched television while waiting to go to his next job.

We kids had our own family gang back then. Our gang was nothing like what I became involved in later; it was just a bunch of neighborhood kids. We ran from house to house and were treated by the adults who lived there as their own. If we needed a swat, we got one. If we needed food, we got it. If we needed a hug or a bandage, we got that too. We loved to play hide-and-seek and marbles, and did gymnastics off the roofs. We loved to ride our bikes no-handed down Francis Street Hill, coasting to see who could get to the bottom fastest. I have a lot of fond memories of a childhood spent with friends and family.

My neighborhood was full of family. My uncle Sonny lived next door, and up the street was my biological father's cousin who had fourteen kids. My mom had eleven siblings, many who lived nearby. My cousins were in and out of the house all the time. We were a wild bunch, racing in and out the doors, eating like crazy, fighting, and making up. My cousins were like my own brothers and sisters, and we were the same to them.

We appreciated my parents' multiple jobs most at Christmas. My mom took this holiday seriously! She didn't give us lots of gifts throughout the year, but she loved to save up and give us stuff at Christmas. She told me she'd buy stuff on sale all year and hide it in the attic.

We loved the decorations, food, and anticipation of the big event, tearing downstairs early in the morning to gape at the gifts under the tree. My mom made us wait to open gifts until we were all up, but the wait was worth it. The best present I remember getting was my first remote control car. I could program in where it would go using a little computer in the car. I loved to watch that car roam around the house, nipping at the heels of my parents and siblings.

> I went to church, had two parents in the home, and had enough to eat. But all that doesn't mean much when a young person begins to be drawn into the darker, more tempting side of life.

I spent a lot of time at my grandparents' house on Caufield Street on the west side of Grand Rapids during the summers and when my mom needed to be gone at night during the school year. My grandparents' house had only one way in, so we had to pass between the TV and my grandfather's chair to get to the rest of the house.

"Get out of my light," he'd holler every time we walked through, which was pretty often during those long summer days. We called him Daddy, the only person I'd ever called Daddy in my childhood. I called Gaylord by his first name from childhood. It wasn't until after he and my mom married, well into my adulthood, that I began to call him Dad.

STARVED FOR TRUTH

I've come to realize that life choices and events happen despite even the most stable upbringing. I went to church, had two parents in the home, and had enough to eat. But all that doesn't mean much when a young person begins to be drawn into the darker, more tempting side of life.

My early school years were typical for our neighborhood. Many of my cousins came to the house before school because my mom in charge of getting us off. We took the bus to Alger Elementary School, and later we walked to Burton Middle School. We were back at my house after school with my older sister usually in charge.

Church wasn't a huge part of our lives. Some of my cousins had no choice but to attend services each week, but we were merely encouraged to attend. My mother insisted she'd never set foot in another church after she'd witnessed the hypocrisy, greed, and lust in the church of her youth. My biological father was a pastor's son, after all. Yet we made the three-minute walk to my grandfather's church as often as possible. I learned about the foundations of faith, was informed often of the consequences of sin, and even attended purity classes designed to teach us about the carnal sins we would face one day soon.

The fall of man and the redeeming power of the living God were discussed often though I didn't fully understand. I came to see God as simply wanting me to perform for him, and if I didn't, God would display his wrath because he was the boss and he could. I concluded that God was a bully, which to me was the weakest display of manhood. I decided I wasn't interested in what God had to offer, but I sure was interested in the treats, activities, and girls.

> I decided I wasn't interested in what God had to offer, but I sure was interested in the treats, activities, and girls. Our church was designed for adults with worship and fellowship couched in the language of adults.

My thinking about God as a giant bully made its way into the classroom. I had a bit of a Robin Hood mentality. I despised bullies and would fight them whenever I thought it necessary, sticking up for kids who were being picked on. One boy, a fifth-grader named Danny, was built like a grown man. He'd get high by picking on anyone he wanted. One day, I'd had enough, so I called him out. He called me a couple of nasty names, and I called him a couple of names; we came face-to-face in the schoolyard, but the bell rang to end recess.

"Why did I do that?" I said to myself. The standoff became the talk of the school that day because no one had ever stood up to Danny. The showdown occurred after school. Danny found me and called me a four-letter word, then we rushed at each other like charging bulls. We ended up on the ground, me in a headlock and Danny's leg clinched in my arms. We might have stayed there for hours but Danny said, "Want to quit?"

I said yes, and we got up and walked away. The next day we became best friends for the duration of our elementary years.

I was much more talented outside the classroom than in it during those school years. I didn't grasp the concept of basic subjects such as reading and math, so I didn't do well academically and seemed incapable of making good choices. One of my bad choices involved a white kid named Craig, someone I thought of as a friend until he called me the "N" word. I waited until the last recess, then ran full speed at him, jumping over a small fence and delivering a furious snap kick to his face.

He dropped, and I was all over him. I hit him until I felt the hands of the principal grabbing my collar. He dragged me across the playground as I kicked and screamed, no one else saying a word. I had to call my mom and explain to her what happened. She was at the school in less than twenty minutes, hollering at the principal and the whole school about what that boy called me. I was in trouble at school for fighting but didn't get in trouble at home (for once).

I admit to being a bit animated in class from third through sixth grades (I'm sure my teachers would call it something else). I goofed off, blew off homework, generally misbehaved as much as possible. Looking back, I probably did that because I struggled so much with reading and math. I couldn't understand either one, so I felt dumb. Somehow I skated through each year until sixth grade, but that grade was another monster altogether.

Ms. Sherman didn't put up with my foolishness at all. I failed every subject, got in trouble, and generally made her and everyone else miserable.

One day, near the end of the year, she sat me down. She wore pearls and a teal-colored shirt. Her breath smelled like coffee as she leaned toward me.

"Troy, you don't deserve to pass sixth grade. But I'm going to pass you to get you out of my face," she said. And she did. I was headed for seventh grade, a much bigger world. I wouldn't do well there either.

My early years influenced me in many ways. In my urban neighborhood, as in many such neighborhoods, danger lurked around every corner. I saw the fancy cars and bling of the drug dealers and envied the gang members' freedom. Dealers were eager to make friends and drum up new customers. Violence was everywhere— gang shootings, murder, drug dealing, prostitution, stabbings, theft.

> I saw the fancy cars and bling of the drug dealers and envied the gang members' freedom. Dealers were eager to make friends and drum up new customers. Violence was everywhere— gang shootings, murder, drug dealing, prostitution, stabbings, theft.

My family experience was not unusual in my neighborhood. There wasn't a lot of supervision because my mom and dad worked, as did many other parents. They were blue-collar workers and kept two jobs each to feed us. We never went hungry physically.

But I did go hungry spiritually. I was starved for answers, yet I wasn't allowed to ask the questions at church or engage in healthy discussions with leaders of the faith. My questions were viewed as rebellious, and the lines of communication were shut down and replaced with nothing but lectures about sin and its consequences. This left me in a place of want and despair—the perfect starting point for life on the streets and gang activity.

I call this "foundational truth malnutrition and starvation."

Some churches offer rules and sermons but not how to really live with the foundational truths of God. I starved in my desire for answers. I filled my spiritual belly with hip-hop dancing, drinking, gangs, and violence.

TAKE IT HOME

Ministries can avoid truth malnutrition and starvation.

1. How can you open your doors to the children and teens in your neighborhood, giving them a safe place to be and safe things to do?

2. Young people have questions and want answers. How can you open the lines of communication? Can you be the place they come to for answers about life and about God?

3. Kids face tough issues every day: pressure to have sex, drink, use drugs, cheat, steal; they have no jobs, no money, no hope for the future. How willing are you to talk about the tough issues? Can you talk honestly and realistically about how to say no? Can you offer life-skills learning opportunities and let them see that living differently is within their grasp?

4. Can you speak the truth with love? You'll want to move beyond the physical and emotional to the spiritual issues—how they relate to others and their world. Talk about the hard stuff—sin, sacrifice, redemption, and forgiveness. And keep talking about it. I wonder how different my life would have been had I gotten answers to some of the questions I had.

2

DREAMS IN THE DARKNESS

Misplaced hope is still powerful.

I could barely read, and math was a mystery. My behavior in school was less than perfect, but I could dance. I could move like the cats in the movies *Breakin'* and *Breakin' Two: Electric Boogaloo*, or at least I thought I could. Maybe I was like the guy who sings in the car or shower and thinks he sounds like a superstar. Regardless of true talent, my dream was to be a hip-hop star.

That's key to a kid—the dream. No matter how realistic (or unrealistic), everyone needs hope. And skill provides very powerful hope.

My skill was hip-hop, which is much more than just a hype dance style. It's more than break dancing or rap music, and has its own subculture with social rules, fashions, heroes, and history. It started in the late 1960s and early '70s in the Bronx borough of New York City. Jamaican disc jockey and musician DJ Kool Herc is considered one of the fathers of the culture, but elements of hip-hop can be seen in the moves of Earl Tucker ("Snake Hips") in the '20s and James Brown in the '60s.

Another big name is Afrika Bambaataa, called the grandfather and godfather of the hip-hop culture (zulunation.com). He birthed new sounds, businesses, and groups centered on hip-hop music. What began as house parties for hip-hop fans became a worldwide movement.

"Bam," as he's called, was one of the leaders who used hip-hop to take the edge off the street gangs that were proliferating during the '60s and '70s. Instead of stabbing and shooting one another, the gangs would battle in the four major hip-hop elements: graffiti, emceeing, deejaying, and breakin' (dancing).

> It wasn't just about the dancing and rapping; it was in the hip-hop environment that I felt welcome, even as a young teen.

One of the most influential moments in hip-hop history occurred when the deejay Grand Wizard Theodore accidentally dropped the needle onto a turning disc (his mom was getting on him about the noise, most likely) and "needle drop," or "scratchin'," was invented. Scratchin' was an immediate success with the deejays and fans and is now an integral part of the hip-hop sound.

BORN TO HIP-HOP

My best friend, Craig Quillin, became the well-known local deejay CraigyQ as we grew older. Together we created mix tapes (hip-hop music with our embellishments) that we brought to the skating rink. The deejays waited for us to bring those tapes, announcing when our music was up. The crowd went wild when they heard our names. We were the top dogs!

I was consumed with the hip-hop culture by age ten. As with most youth in those days, Michael Jackson was my hero. I had a makeshift white glove and looked for a pair of flood pants. I loved dancing, but eventually dabbled in the other three elements. But it wasn't just about the dancing and rapping; it was in the hip-hop environment that I felt welcome, even as a young teen.

I started sneaking into the 8-Ball to watch the dancers by the time I was twelve. The pool hall occupied the main floor, but downstairs was a small room where the greatest breakers went to battle. The room was dark, smoky, and underground—a mirror of the hip-hop movement in those days. I loved that atmosphere as a near-teenager, getting close to the alcohol, cigarettes, drugs, and women.

What I loved more was the acceptance I found there. There was no racial or gang tension in that dark room. A group of white dudes with a crew (dance team) would come down, but their skin color didn't matter. What mattered was what they could do on the floor. The lack of racial tension is just one example of the acceptance so many found in the hip-hop culture and still find today.

The only thing I thought I could do well was be me. I couldn't do school, couldn't do church. But I could be me on that piece of cardboard laid down for dancing on a cold cement floor. And I was accepted for being me.

I watched the dancers' breakin' moves in amazement, then went home and pretended I was them. I got my own cardboard and tried to dance, walk, and talk like they did. I had to dress the hip-hop part, too. Parachute or army pants, a tank top, windbreaker, and bandana was my uniform. Some of the cats wore hats to protect their heads, from tams or Green Beret hats to baseball caps or knit winter caps. The jewelry came later, when rap became more prevalent. Today I laugh a little at the baggy pants the young dudes wear. We didn't wear those back in the day because, frankly, we'd have been dancing in our drawers! Our pants had to stay up when we were wowing crowds with our breakin' skills.

ACCEPTANCE AND MORE

People at the 8-Ball accepted me despite my dismal record. They were cool! They dressed, talked, and danced cool. I loved the throbbing music, dancing, atmosphere, and contests. I also loved that there was nobody telling me what to do and how to act. There were certain standards in the hip-hop world, but they were standards I could live up to.

> I loved the throbbing music, dancing, atmosphere, and contests. I also loved that there was nobody telling me what to do and how to act. There were certain standards in the hip-hop world, but they were standards I could live up to.

This world was so different from the church world I knew. There were no lectures and lists of things I couldn't and shouldn't do. There were no stern adults pointing out all the things I was doing wrong. I didn't sense the racial, economic, and social tensions so much a part of that time.

Everyone in the local hip-hop world looked forward all year to the Grand Rapids Arts Festival, held in downtown Grand Rapids each June. Food booths dotted the streets for blocks; stages were set up all over downtown for performances, though not for my kind of music. We met in less formal settings, such as street corners and alleys. Hip-hop dance crews from all over Michigan came to the city to battle it out—not with knives and guns but with boom boxes and six-by-six-foot pieces of cardboard. The groups walked around looking for the next battle. When they found one, they'd throw the cardboard on the ground, turn on the music, and dance like crazy.

I remember seeing a battle with some older guys when I was eleven or twelve. A stocky guy wearing army pants started dancing, and he could move like Ozone in *Breakin'*. He was so good that he shut down the session; his competition just backed away.

We started talking, and he mentioned that his grandfather lived in Grand Rapids and had a church just down the street. We both turned and looked at the church, visible from the corner of Division Street and Griggs Avenue. I said that was funny because my grandfather had a church down the street too. I pointed to the same church.

Turns out he was one of four half-brothers, sons of my birth father, who I knew nothing about. Richard was about fourteen at the time we met. He and his brothers Titus and Mark were in one family; my brother Mark and I in another, and another son, Markus, in another. We grew up three miles apart. (I still see Richard and Titus fairly often, as well as my other half-siblings.)

Another place we loved to dance was the Madison Street Fair, held each year in my neighborhood. There was food, kids' activities, and a talent presentation that allowed me, my cousin Rob, and my pro-tégé Terrell to battle with other dance groups. It was at the Madison Street Fair that I met Bill McKinney, a dancer from Chicago who would become a huge influence on my life. Bill, or B-Mack, asked me if I'd like to form a dance group and, with that, the All-Star Dancers was born.

> There was always a need to be "that guy." The coolest of the cool, the best of the best. We all struggled to get to the top and would do just about anything to get there.

As I became immersed in the hip-hop culture, even at such a young age, I began to see its underside. Sure, the clothes were dope; the dancing was great; and the ear-splitting, head-pounding beat was mesmerizing.

But there was always a need to be "that guy." The coolest of the cool, the best of the best. We all struggled to get to the top and would do just about anything to get there. That desire to be cool led to some pretty rough stuff. Drugs and alcohol were present, and sexual perversion was a part of the culture.

With the drugs came the money, and with the money came the girls. Everybody tapped into the scene, both making money and spending it. If you weren't buying dope, you were selling it. Girls were abused; they sold themselves for drug money or, sometimes, food money, or for merely spending time with them. Dudes attacked each other over who owed who money, the girls, or some imagined slight.

Alcoholism was the norm. Everybody drank. I had my first drink at age fourteen. I thought drinking was beneath me at first, but everybody was doing it so I tried it just once. I tried it again a few weeks later, and that time, I didn't stop.

WORLD OF DARKNESS

Despite all of that, I'm convinced that urban culture is not bad at its core and not without hope of redemption. Just as with other cultures—the country club crowd, private school culture, theater culture, and so on—the urban culture has been under attack and exploited by evil. Evil forces readily use the violence, poverty, and drugs so prevalent there for their own ends.

So why was I so enamored by the hip-hop lifestyle? The drugs, violence, and promiscuity are socially counterproductive and spiritually depleting. What was the allure to a young boy who had a relatively stable home life, parents and family who loved him, enough food, and a place to stay?

That's easy: I was trying to prove I was a man. More than just being "the man," I wanted to be a man. The dancing, violence, drinking, and girls were about that one thing. My descent into the world of violence and promiscuity began when I was sexually abused at age nine.

TAKE IT HOME

Reaching into the Culture

Mature Christian adults tend to shy away from the youth and hip-hop culture. They did when I was a boy and still do today. Their absence leaves a vacuum that should be filled by an older generation trying to educate and moderate the hip-hop influence. That generation, engaged in the culture, can earn the right to say, "It's OK to dance, but this is where you need to stop."

Here are a few suggestions for engaging the culture:

1. Be among Them. Hang out with them, open your home, visit the places they visit. Kids will open their world to you when they know you truly care and are interested. How can you express authentic care when you disapprove?

2. Do Incarnational Ministry. That is, be transparent with the people in the culture; participate in the culture, but avoid its pitfalls; work for justice where necessary; be generous, hospitable, and creative. What are some of the barriers that stop you from engaging a particular culture?

3. Learn from the Culture. Those in the hip-hop world have much to teach us about acceptance, loyalty, and love. I call this honoring indigenous wisdom. What are some examples of opening your mind to considering that people in the hip-hop culture might know something? How can you avoid forcing your ways on the people?

Defining Terms

Hip-Hop—A culture that encompasses a primarily urban lifestyle, fashion, language, and music. Hip-hop traditionally includes four elements: deejaying, graffiti, emceeing, and dancing. Known as a culture of the streets.

Rap—A musical genre that rhymes to a beat; heavily influenced by hip-hop, though much of it has pulled away from its hip-hop roots.

Graffiti—A visual aspect of hip-hop; a form of art and expression often done on buildings, buses, trains, etc., most often with spray paint; often considered vandalism, but also a viable form of self-expression by many in the urban culture.

DJ—The one spinning CDs and albums; the one who keeps the music coming and party rolling; often uses high-tech equipment, though early DJs used turntables.

Breakdancing, or Breakin'—The dance moves of hip-hop, often reflecting martial arts and fighting moves; the unique dancing that evolved from the urban culture.

Emceeing—Chanting rhyming lyrics; often referred to as rapping, which combines song, poetry, and beat.

DESECRATION

Redeeming the abused requires seeing the abuse.

We spent a lot of time at my grandmother's house during the summers. With both of my parents working long hours, we often went to the west side of Grand Rapids to be babysat by my loving grandma. My cousins were often there as well, so we had quite a gang of kids running around their small yard.

My grandmother was the most solid Christian I ever knew. She was strong in her faith and so strong for other people. She stood firm in the midst of trials, always willing to lend a hand or share her wisdom. I knew she loved me and my siblings and cousins. She was loving but firm, not letting us get away with talking back to her, badmouthing others, or behaving badly.

Those were good days for us. I remember hanging around the yard as my uncles sat on the porch singing old Motown songs from the Temptations and Smokey Robinson, groups like Cameo, and R&B stuff from Earth, Wind & Fire. Guitars came out and my uncle Dave Jacobs (who they called Cameo) would jump on the drums; the Detrick brothers would sing and play.

All of us kids needed each other on those long, hot days. I don't remember too many toys or games at her house (and my grandfather used the television most of the time), so we had to make up things to do. Announcing we were bored was my grandmother's cue to holler, "Go outside!" Out we'd troop to organize races around the block or play tag or hide-and-seek. We'd pick mulberries when they were in season, washing them off and covering them in sugar for a snack. There's nothing like a handpicked, sugar-covered handful of mulberries on a warm day!

INNOCENCE

Our friends Wanda and Joy lived next door with their parents. Wanda and Joy were part of our gang, so to speak, and involved in any races and games we played. They had two siblings, Al and Tammy, who were six or seven years older than us. Al was a different dude, always acted a little strange. But he was fun and made time to play with us kids.

He would organize our round-the-block races and facilitate push-up contests. One time my cousin Kenny Jacobs (who is also my god-brother) wasn't doing his push-ups correctly, so Al grabbed him by the loop of his pants and hoisted him up and down to demonstrate proper push-up style. As I remember it, Al dropped Kenny, and he chipped his front tooth.

One especially hot day, Al offered to be our human horse. He lined us all up and, one by one, sat us on his shoulders and went running around the block. We all eagerly waited our turn, happy to sit on his sweaty shoulders for a new view of the neighborhood and a race around the block. Al sure seemed to enjoy it all as much as the rest of us.

Then it was my turn, and I was ready to go! He picked me up and put me on his shoulders and off we went. I'd never ridden a horse before, but if it was half as fun as this I decided I needed to get one for myself.

The trip came to a halt when Al stopped at an old green garage. Peeling paint and junk were everywhere, trash covering the ground. The inside smelled like urine. He asked me if I had to go to the bathroom. I did, so I undid my pants and headed to a corner of the garage.

But I felt eyes watching me. I twisted around and saw Al staring at me, standing right next to me. He reached down and I felt him touch me. To this day, I don't remember the specifics of what happened there. But I remember his stinky skin, ugly eyes, and sour breath.

I knew that what he did was wrong. I couldn't stop him.

We left the garage and returned to the other kids. But I was done playing. I went into my grandmother's house and sat down. I was angry, confused, and felt guilty. I was sure I'd done something wrong. All I'd wanted was to ride the human horse. I didn't have any words in my vocabulary for what had happened to me—it was beyond my understanding.

Of course my grandmother didn't notice anything strange about my behavior, or at least didn't ask me whether anything had happened.

I never said a word about the incident. I couldn't. I was ashamed that I had let it happen, confused at why Al touched me, and so very afraid that I was the abnormal one. It never occurred to me that Al was to blame.

VIOLATED

The longer I kept silent about the sexual abuse, the more rage I felt. The rage weighed heavier and heavier; my anger became deeper and deeper. Years later, as a young man, I still wouldn't be able to deal with this alone. Yet I would remain embarrassed to admit anything happened because I was embarrassed at my response to the abuse at the time. I know now I responded physically as any boy would. Still, I couldn't realize that my response was merely physical; my body couldn't have behaved any differently. My physical response had nothing to do with who I was on the inside. I worried that I was a homosexual because I had been molested by a man.

To my nine-year-old mind, I was stripped of my masculinity and identity. "Who am I?" was my question for years. I may not have known who I was, but I sure knew who I wouldn't be. I knew that I wouldn't sit back and let anyone bully or punk me ever again. I didn't care who it was—kid my age, neighborhood teenager, adult. No one would ever again be able to do or say whatever they wanted to me.

I would be in full control of my destiny from this moment on. And no one would ever take advantage of anyone I cared for, either.

Those vows would change my life forever.

To this day, I often wonder who else might have fallen victim to this man's perverse trap. His younger sisters? My own siblings and cousins? Other neighborhood kids? Surely I wasn't the first, and I likely wasn't the last. I also wonder how many other boys have been abused by adults they trusted. My mom had been proactive in discussing sexual abuse with the girls in our family, which was indeed a good thing. But I don't think too many adults have that discussion with boys. At least they didn't in my family.

As any child does, I had my crushes—girls I liked but didn't say anything to; girls I thought were cute. Typical kid stuff. I had a crush on one of my mom's best friends, a woman named Vaneeta. I was twelve at the time, and she was in her late twenties. I thought of her as some kind of African queen, the dream girlfriend for me. She was always nice to me and commented on how handsome I was. Of course I got all fuzzy, and when she left our house, my cousins and I talked about how pretty she was.

When I was about twenty—I was "on top of my game" and involved in the gangs, drinking, and crime—I bumped into her at a wedding. I asked her to dance, and she then invited me to her house for the night. While we were together, she whispered, "I've been wanting you since you were a kid."

STATS

Approximately 60 percent of boys and 80 percent of girls who have been abused were abused by someone the child knows.

According to the Adverse Childhood Experiences Study of the Centers for Disease Control and Prevention, 20.7 percent of adults have experienced some kind of sexual abuse (http://www.cdc.gov/nccdphp/ace/prevalence.htm).

According to the Child Health USA 2006 survey, 1.2 percent of every one thousand children experience some sort of childhood sexual abuse (www.mchb.hrsa.gov/chusa_06/healthstat/children/graphs/0314can.htm).

—From Prevent Child Abuse America
http://www.preventchildabuse.org/advocacy/downloads/child_sexual_abuse.pdf

General Warning Signs of Sexual Abuse
- Nightmares or other sleep problems without explanation
- Seems distracted or distant at times
- Sudden change in eating habits (increased or decreased appetite; trouble swallowing)
- Mood swings: rage, fear, insecurity, withdrawal
- Writes, draws, plays, or dreams of sexual or frightening images
- New or unusual fear of certain people or places
- Refuses to talk about a secret shared with an adult or older child
- Talks about a new older friend
- Has money, toys, or gifts without reason
- Thinks of self or body as repulsive or bad
- Exhibits adult-like sexual behaviors, language, or knowledge

In Younger Children
- An older child behaving like a younger child (thumb sucking, bed wetting)
- New words for private body parts
- Resists removing clothes when appropriate (bath, bed, toileting, diapering)
- Asks other children to behave sexually or play sexual games
- Mimics adult-like behaviors with toys or stuffed animals
- Wetting or soiling accidents unrelated to toilet training

In Adolescents
- Self-injury (cutting, burning)
- Inadequate personal hygiene
- Drug and alcohol abuse
- Sexual promiscuity
- Running away from home
- Depression, anxiety, suicide attempts
- Fear of intimacy or closeness
- Compulsive eating or dieting

—From Stop It Now!
http://www.stopitnow.com/warning_signs_child_behavior

I'm not sure how she thought this would make me feel, but I was extremely disturbed. Even in my drunken stupor I felt that same, violated feeling I felt as a child when Al molested me in the garage. I was so upset that I got up and left, walking home in the rain at three in the morning.

The worst part is that this time everybody knew what happened. My whole family attended that wedding and watched me leave with this older woman. My brothers and cousins even cheered me on! But I'll never forget the look on my mama's face when I showed up on her porch the next morning. I had hurt her deeply.

The strangest thing is that I had let this happen, was even eager to let it happen. Having sex with this older woman brought on the same feelings I had when I was molested by that young man all those years ago. I had the same feelings of shame, guilt, and regret.

TAKE IT HOME

Ministries that are going to relevantly engage the cultures of their communities have to realize and be sensitive to the brokenness that exists under the surface. There are never simplistic reasons or cause-and-effect scenarios, but many who abuse people in one form or another were initiated by being abused themselves when young. Fears of and hatred against homosexuality, for instance, can come out of latent fears ingrained by abuse in childhood. And sexual aberrations in predators within a community can often be traced back to when the predator was prey.

Christians, of all people, should be able to appreciate the bitter reality of sins passed from one generation to the next. But they also know how God's grace can break the cycle and redeem the broken. Ministries need to do more than whistle in the dark and pretend the awkward and offensive evils against children will somehow go away. Healing and restoration can come about by acknowledging and confronting the sin of violation against another. Careful counseling and God's supernatural grace are powerful tools in the face of such daunting destruction.

Ministries can also help prevent sexual abuse within their walls and on sponsored events by taking basic precautions such as these:

1. The Six-Month Rule. Volunteer youth, children's, or nursery workers must attend the church for at least six months prior to being allowed to work with children or teens.

2. Screen All Workers. Have all volunteers fill out an application before working with youth, then run a background check on each one. Investigate any possible problems, and contact all references listed on the application.

3. Two Adults Always. Never allow a child to be alone with one adult either on or off the ministry campus. All ages need two adults present in the room, vehicle, or off-campus site.

4. Non-Family Rule. Those two adults shouldn't be from the same extended family, if possible, and definitely not from the same immediate family.

5. Restroom Time. Take groups of children to the restroom at a time, accompanied by several adults. Leave the restroom door open, though make sure passersby can't see into stalls.

6. Check-In. Create a check-in procedure to ensure children are released only to a parent, guardian, or authorized person.

7. Mentoring. Make sure one-on-one mentoring is done in appropriate settings and at appropriate times.

8. Abuse Watch. Train workers to look for signs of sexual (or other forms of) abuse in the children and youth they work with.

9. Volunteer Behavior. Train workers and staff to look for signs of inappropriate behavior in volunteers, such as trying to isolate themselves with one individual.

10. Safe Haven. Offer a safe place for children and teens to go if they experience sexual abuse at home, school, church, or other places.

11. Report All Abuse. Sexual abuse is punishable by law.

4

PREY TO PREDATOR

The cycle of sin continues when we don't care less.

I was doomed from the start. School and I just didn't get along, and that meant one of us had to go. I made it through my second year of seventh grade before being sent to Stockbridge. The name makes it sound like a prison, but it was an alternative school full of kids and young adults who couldn't achieve in traditional school settings. The school had its own smoking room with a pool table for the students.

I was a small guy and no one knew me, so I got picked on first. I remember being mean mugged at school by dudes with full beards! My background, however, was a little different than they had expected. My mom has a green belt in karate, and her oldest brother could bench press more than three hundred pounds despite the fact that he only weighed slightly more than half that. My older sister was a street brawler men feared. My brother was a second-degree black belt; two of my cousins next door were green belts. Not to mention that I knew boxing. Our family was prepared for the fight.

FIGHTER

My aunt is sister to world-class boxing trainer Floyd Mayweather, Sr., which makes world champion Floyd Mayweather, Jr. her nephew. We often jogged up to the now-defunct Pride Boxing Gym and worked out with Buster Mathis, Sr., the heavyweight boxer who turned pro in 1965. He won thirty fights and lost four (to Joe Frazier, Jerry Quarry, Muhammad Ali, and Ron Lyle) before retiring in Grand Rapids to train other boxers, including his son Buster Mathis, Jr. Mathis, Sr. died in 1995 in Grand Rapids. I was on a weight-lifting regimen by age eleven, and in my first year of seventh grade won the city championship in wrestling.

> I was on a weight-lifting regimen by age eleven, and in my first year of seventh grade won the city championship in wrestling.

But those dudes at Stockbridge School didn't know all that—especially a scratchy-bearded dude named Sean. He was well-known for fighting anyone and was the ultimate bully. I was committed to not getting into trouble at this new school because I really wanted to succeed there. Then Sean tried to punk me. I let him talk at me and call me names; I would respond with, "You just better not put your hands on me."

This went on for about a month until a cold winter morning. The ground was slick with ice as everyone walked into the building. Sean ran up to me, raised his fists to fight, and said, "What's up now?" I sized him up and studied his stance, knowing immediately that he wasn't a skilled fighter. His feet were too far apart, he was standing flat footed, and his left leg was way too exposed.

"I do not want to fight you," I said, looking him in the eye. I was shaking on the inside as I turned to walk away. I heard footsteps behind me and people commenting on what a punk I was. This must have fueled Sean, because he jumped in front of me and took a swing, nicking my face. I did a fake punch and shot in to do a single-leg takedown, slamming him head first onto the ice.

I realized what I had done and immediately started to walk away. He got up and tried to swing again, but this time I caught his arm and chicken-winged him. His feet went flying and he was slammed to the ice once again. I was done talking. I stood in my fighting stance and waited for him to get up so I could beat him down again. He stood slowly, a confused look on his face. I called him a couple of four-letter words and told him in so many words that his butt was mine. I was on my way to rush him when the security guard snatched me up.

I was suspended and shortly afterward dropped out without even the most basic skills. I later found out that I read at about a second-grade level.

PRIDE AND LUST

I was one prideful dude. I refused to ask for help because I didn't want anyone to think I was dumb. I suspect now that I had some learning disabilities, but in those days and in those schools, such things weren't much cared for or cared about.

Despite my disastrous academic record, my record with the ladies was A+. I was top of the class in that department. At about age ten, not long after the sexual abuse, I became obsessed with the opposite sex. I discovered quickly that when I turned on the charm, I commanded the attention of the girls around me.

School became my personal charm school. I spent lots of time talking to girls, teasing them, trying to get their attention. Certain of my charms worked on some girls, other of my charming traits worked on others. My goal was to be the center of attention, to have all the girls at my beck and call. My real goal, of course, was to prove I was a "man." The sexual abuse loomed over me always in the back of my mind. I felt I needed to prove something. Though I told no one about it, I still needed to prove something, mostly to myself.

> My goal was to be the center of attention, to have all the girls at my beck and call. My real goal, of course, was to prove I was a "man."

At age eleven, when most boys were playing basketball, building forts, or playing video games, I was messing around with Chrissy. She was several years older than me, but she had been sexually involved with older guys for some time. For weeks we had played around sexually.

But that wasn't enough for Chrissy. She invited me to meet her in a broken-down garage to have sex with her. I was scared to death, excited, curious, and intimidated all at the same time. Of course I put on a brave face, but really I just wanted her to like me.

That abandoned garage—smelly, dark, and damp—became the place I squandered my gift of virginity at age eleven. The sad reality of that experience was that we were two little kids just looking for something that we had no clue how to obtain.

When she extended that invitation to go to the garage, my feelings were twofold: First, that she obviously loved me because of what we had been doing and what she would soon allow to happen. Second, I figured that to prove I loved her I'd have to do something to solidify my position in her heart. My hope was that by participating in this sexual act, I could somehow cook up the needed materials to make "love."

I don't know exactly what Chrissy was looking for—probably the same things I was—but I found out later that she had been involved with grown men who had stolen her innocence from her. She probably didn't know anything different: sex equaled love, and she was looking for love through sex.

Underneath all of my bravado and interest in girls and sex, I was simply fighting the thought that I had been molested and needed to "prove" I was a man. I decided that I would prove my manhood by having sex with as many girls as possible. In the sixth grade, my cousin and I started a tally of the girls we kissed and had sex with. We were racing to see who could get to one hundred first.

Combine a failing school record with a huge interest in girls and what do you get? Skipping school to have sex, of course. I had it all figured out. I'd leave my parents' home in the morning like I was going to school, but I'd bypass school and head over to a girl's house and spend the day in sexual pursuits.

By age fourteen, I had more sexual experience than a lot of guys ever have. I often drew the eye of older females. We didn't think about the consequences of our actions—pregnancy, sexually transmitted diseases, HIV/AIDS, getting caught—only about what we thought was making ourselves happy.

> We didn't think about the consequences of our actions—pregnancy, sexually transmitted diseases, HIV/AIDS, getting caught— only about what we thought was making ourselves happy.

SEXUALIZED LIES

I was pretty proud as I made a name for myself in the hip-hop culture that I loved. My actions were prompted by several things: the sexual abuse, obviously, but also the sexualized world of hip-hop. Over the years, hip-hop grew from a platform for the young to speak out about difficult issues in the late 1960s and '70s into a major industry. Hip-hop started being controlled or pimped by the men in corporate offices. Rappers abandoned the idea of "keeping it real" to follow the call of the mighty dollar.

Through its songs, videos, and provocative dance styles, the "new and improved" hip-hop culture presented a message to youth that perverted sexuality but made it seem normal.

So-called hip-hop gangsters and pimps were surrounded by beautiful women, or at least it seemed so in the videos, glossy magazines, and television clips. The women were provocatively dressed and full of moves that would make a prostitute blush. The men drove the most expensive cars and were draped in "blingage."

The battle of being a normal kid chasing the golden dream was that I could not just talk the talk. Or so I thought. I listened to what every gangster rapper would tell me: that I could kill police officers, sell drugs, and pimp the ladies. It started blurring my picture of reality. They started to draw me into the snares of the hijacked hip-hop lifestyle by any means necessary! I say hijacked because I do not believe that where hip-hop has ended up is where it was meant to be.

For young dudes it's about being dangerous or violent and a "playa." For girls it's about the perfect body and being open to sexual advances. Girls went from Queen Latifah shouting "Ladies First" in the late 1980s to readily agreeing to being called four-letter words and using their bodies to get what they want from men. And the men parrot the often misogynistic lyrics to songs that degrade women, creating a strange division of love/hate, cool/uncool, respect/disrespect that presents mixed messages to young people.

TURNING A BLIND EYE

Those mixed messages were so much a part of my life as a young teenager that I found it impossible to discern the truth. I wanted to prove I was a man, but I also just wanted to be liked. I wanted to find love, but took only sex. I wanted to be cool, but my actions were often mean and degrading. And I found no answers through the church. I wasn't looking, but the church wasn't reaching out to me, either.

My experiences with sex and the hip-hop culture and my attitudes toward both mirror much of what is still going on today. Today's youth experience those same mixed messages as they listen to trashy song lyrics, dance seductively, and embrace the violence and sexualized urban culture. Ministries and churches stand apart and don't want to get involved because they perceive hip-hop as guilty because of its association with sex and violence.

> I found no answers through the church. I wasn't looking, but the church wasn't reaching out to me, either.

The bottom line is that we must give our youth their identity; if we don't, the streets will. So many of us walk around in circles for years, looking for our identity, calling, and purpose. Yet God, in his infinite wisdom, created all of us—young people included—with all three of those things. Check out these verses that speak to identity, purpose, and calling:

- Ephesians 2:10: "We are God's workmanship, created in Christ Jesus to do good works, which God prepared in advance for us to do."
- Psalm 139:13–14: "For you created my inmost being; you knit me together in my mother's womb. I praise you because I am fearfully and wonderfully made; your works are wonderful, I know that full well."

TAKE IT HOME

Ministries and concerned adults can do several things to help youth take a good look at and begin to discern the real truth behind the mixed messages of the hip-hop culture.

1. Teach Media Literacy. Youth see only what the media and hip-hop stars want them to see. Kids see only the best photo ops, the stars dressed up and blinged out, the most beautiful women. But those photos and videos present only one highly staged moment. Encourage youth to understand that these are staged, often air-brushed, photos that don't represent truth. Teach them that MTV, BET, and VH1 videos are not how life really is.

2. Teach the Difference between Sex and Love. True love has nothing to do with sex, and having sex doesn't equal love. Help urban-culture youth (and all youth, for that matter) discern the difference.

3. Encourage Appropriate Self-Esteem. A young man's self-esteem should be based on his role as God's beloved child, not how he looks in baggy pants and a big gold necklace. A girl's self-esteem should be based on her place as God's daughter, not as the sexualized plaything of young men.

4. Teach the Difference between Reality and Fantasy. The hip-hop culture and its stars easily move between fantasy and reality in their music and videos. In a young person's mind, the fantasy of a big car and lots of money, often achieved through violence, easily beats the reality of poverty, no job skills, or abuse of alcohol. Help young people dig deep to discover where they are living in fantasy and refocus on the reality of life and the things they need to do to succeed (graduate from high school, attend college, save money, etc.).

5. Rethink Definitions of Masculinity and Femininity. The urban culture often portrays masculinity as being tough, violent, abusive, and profane. Femininity is often portrayed as seductive, cheap, and sexualized. The Bible offers a completely different view.

6. Choose Appropriate Role Models. Hip-hop stars are not often the best role models for young people. Help them research the stars' lifestyles to discover how they truly live and to decide whether they are appropriate role models. Look for different role models, such as youth leaders, teachers, or other adults.

5

BLOOD IS THICKER

Instruments of redemption realize the power of family.

My family was everywhere. My cousins practically lived at my house and I at their houses. My uncle lived next door. Other aunts and uncles lived in the same neighborhood. I attended school and church with cousins and second cousins, hung out with them after school, and got in trouble alongside them.

I knew some of my half-brothers as well, the sons of my birth father, Mark Morgan. Those were strange relationships. We weren't sure how to act around each other, sensing that the circumstances weren't our fault but not clear on how to navigate our shared father.

> I give a lot of credit to my dad and mom for putting up with me, raising all of us, and working hard to support us. My cousins, siblings, and I were raised as brothers and sisters.

At the center of my world was my mom, Linda Evans, and the man I considered my dad, Gaylord Love.

Dad—who I always called Gaylord until I gave my life to Christ— worked to provide for all of us, loved us, and punished us when we needed it. I give a lot of credit to my dad and mom for putting up with me, raising all of us, and working hard to support us. My cousins, siblings, and I were raised as brothers and sisters.

FAMILY STICKS TOGETHER

I was especially close to my cousin Vern, nicknamed both Choach and Concern; we were thick as thieves. Vern's mama, Barbra, is my mother's younger sister. Vern's family lived with us for a time while they prepared to move.

The two of us attended Alger Elementary School together and loved to wear our penny loafers, flood pants, and white socks. We were all about dressing like our idol, Michael Jackson. We also chased girls together.

Vern was a serious basketball fanatic. He'd create a hoop from a hanger, using his balled-up socks as a basketball as he imagined his way straight to the NBA. The guy kept meticulous statistics of his favorite players in a notebook under his bed. His height and big feet helped his game, which was pretty phenomenal.

Vern and I loved to dance. We'd get special invites to parties because of our Morris Day and The Time imitation. Their song "Jungle Love" would come on, and Vern and I would slip and slide all over the place. One night we were at a party at my uncle Sonny's house, but decided to sneak out and walk around the corner. Vern ended up playing some intense basketball in his penny loafers. Our usual mode of operation was for Vern to totally smash people on the court while I sat on the sideline talking trash.

That night Vern stepped away from the court for a minute, leaving me with a group of angry, frustrated dudes. I was still laughing at them when a big, cross-eyed guy named Steve told me to shut up. I was outnumbered and scared, so I turned to walk away. But Steve followed, taking a swing and connecting. I moved to my fighting stance and threw a couple of kicks (in my penny loafers); then he rushed me like a bull. I was trying to choke him when I felt indescribable pain from my toes to my waist. Cross-eyed Steve had grabbed my "family jewels."

There I was, screaming like a girl in a horror flick when I glimpsed Vern hopping full speed on one foot, his size 12.5 penny loafer in one hand. He started to bust Steve in the head with that shoe until Steve finally let go and started running away.

> My word was golden, which got us in trouble more than once.

Vern and I got into more than just fights. Though we were only a few months apart in age, he always looked to me as an older brother. My word was golden, which got us in trouble more than once. One night I decided I needed to make chocolate chip cookies. I had learned to cook early because of so many kids in the house and having babysitters all the time. I sure wanted those cookies, but we didn't have enough change between us to buy chocolate chips at the local grocery store. I started trash talking to Vern about those chips, telling him about how easy it was to steal from the store and how often I'd done it.

Vern walked right over and took those chips, putting them inside his burgundy jacket. We started walking out fast, but an Asian man, probably the storeowner, grabbed Vern by the coat. Vern jerked away and those chocolate chips went flying everywhere.

"Go get my daddy!" Vern screamed.

I ran out of the store to do just that, thinking to myself, "But his daddy is in Georgia."

His mom found out about the incident and that was the last I saw of Vern—my cousin, brother, and friend—for a few years. When we became adults I told Vern that I'd never stolen anything in my life.

My cousins were a huge part of my life. Kenny Jacobs (nicknamed Wu) is a younger cousin I call my brother and my only god-brother. That boy would do whatever he could to frustrate a person; if something got on your nerves, he'd do it. Maurice, another cousin, lived next door my entire childhood. We loved to do flips off porches, over fences, off garages, and down the middle of the street. Maurice, while not a great break dancer, was off the charts when it came to flips.

He had a move that drew a crowd every time. We called it the "suicide." Maurice would start rocking, psyching himself for the move, then take off running. He'd do a no-handed flip—often on concrete—and land directly on his back. The move had to hurt, but Maurice never said a word. He just looked cool as he got up and walked away.

> But it was my brother Mark, who we called Shark, who was my true hero.

My fellow hustler was Mike Stone, a second cousin on my biological father's side. We'd do anything to get a dollar, including rake leaves, deliver papers, shovel snow, and collect bottles. After a long day of hustling for money, we'd walk about a mile to Popeye's Chicken and buy our favorite treat: a dozen Popeye's biscuits and two large red pops. A fine reward for a hard day's work!

But it was my brother Mark, who we called Shark, who was my true hero. He was the most physically fit preteen you ever saw. While I was chasing girls, Mark was running laps. He was the best wrestler in the hood, never losing a match. We didn't fight and hardly every argued; as long as I stayed out of his stuff, we were cool.

Until I didn't. Mark had made some cookies, and I wanted some. I asked for a few at least twenty times, but he said no every time. I asked again. He gave me the meanest look and told me to sit down. I did, but snuck out a hand to take a few off his plate. Without even looking up, he punched me in the jaw. I put the cookie back; I couldn't have chewed it anyway.

While Mark and I got along fine, my older sister Lisa and I had a love/hate relationship. She taught me everything I needed to know about life, hustling, and cooking; and she was fun to hang out with. But when I got smart with her, she'd fight me like I was a man on the street. I'd often run next door for protection. She'd beat me down at any moment, but nobody else better try anything on me.

> I started sneaking out of the house at night when I was about fourteen. I'd stay out until the early hours of the morning doing all kinds of things.

I remember an incident at my grand-mother's house. I was maybe eleven when a high school dude decided to use my face as a baseball. He swung a yellow, full-size plastic bat right at my face. I started screaming and Lisa starting swinging. She attacked that dude with fists and let him have it, cussing him out while she beat the tar out of him.

I didn't really know my younger sister and brother, who are ten and thirteen years younger than me. I was long gone from the house when they were kids, though I'd stop by to see them because I wanted to know them. We became much better friends when they got older.

I started sneaking out of the house at night when I was about fourteen. I'd stay out until the early hours of the morning doing all kinds of things, from spending nights at girls' houses to hanging out with my friends.

STATS

- 63 percent of youth suicides are from fatherless homes (U.S. Dept. of Health/Census).
- 90 percent of all homeless/runaway children are fatherless.
- 80 percent of rapists are without fathers.
- 71 percent of all high school dropouts are without fathers in the home (National Principals Association Report).
- 85 percent of youth in prison are fatherless.

Ephesians 6:4: "Fathers, do not provoke your children to anger by the way you treat them. Rather, bring them up with the discipline and instruction that comes from the Lord" (NLT).

When I eventually stumbled home, I'd throw pebbles at the window of the bedroom Mark and I shared. He would wake up, come downstairs, and let me in. We were careful to never wake my parents. Mark would fuss at me under his breath, but he never told my mom and dad about my little secret. I would sleep for a couple of hours, then get up and start the process over again. Several times I had to spend the night on the front porch because my brother didn't wake up.

SURROGATES

I told myself that I was slicker than "black ice." I had it all under control with the ladies, my parents, and just about everything. Until one night when the door unlocked as usual. I expected my brother Mark, but instead I faced a six-foot-two-inch, 260-pound black man. Dad had figured me out.

> As much as Dad stepped in to parent me and my siblings, I still had a hole in my heart left by my birth dad that I never understood.

He didn't fuss under his breath like Mark did; he let me have it! I was punished, lectured, grounded, and sent to bed.

The first few times Dad caught me, I was afraid of the punishment. But the more I wanted to be out on my own, the easier the punishments were to handle.

As much as Dad stepped in to parent me and my siblings, I still had a hole in my heart left by my birth dad that I never understood. I saw my biological father maybe three times in my childhood. He had abandoned my mom when he was done with her, moving on to other women and other children.

I admit now that it was a bit of a heart tug to know, in the back of my mind, that my dad was not the man who "made" me. Trying to understand the idea that my birth father didn't want me was a bit much for me.

I had a father and other men in my life (including Pedro, father of my best friend, Craig) who showed me love and were available to me, but there was still a missing piece in my heart that even today I cannot explain. I desired to know and have a relationship with a man who did not desire to know me.

TAKE IT HOME

The family is critical in all communities, but in our urban centers and specifically in the African-American context, we are fighting against generations of division in the home. I believe the role of the man has been intentionally stripped away in the black community, a stripping that began on the slave ships coming from Africa. Male slaves were separated from their families, leaving children with no male figure to give them direction or identity and often leaving the mother bitter and unprotected.

A speech delivered by William Lynch in 1712 on how to "make a slave" unmasks a plan to conquer and divide that we still see in our communities today. Lynch, a British slave owner in the West Indies, had been invited to the colony of Virginia to share his methods with slave owners there. The term *lynching* is allegedly derived from his last name.

I use fear, distrust and envy for control. . . . We have reversed the relationship; in her natural uncivilized state, she would have a strong dependency on the uncivilized . . . male, and she would have a limited protective tendency toward her independent male offspring and would raise male offspring to be dependent like her. . . . For fear of the young male's life, she will psychologically train him to be mentally weak and dependent, but physically strong. Because she has become psychologically independent, she will train her female offspring to be psychologically independent. What have you got? You've got the . . . woman out front and the . . . man behind and scared.[1]

It's apparent how Lynch's legacy continues to plague the African-American culture to this day. Slavery has had a lasting effect on the urban communities we serve. It is critical that ministries, especially in an urban setting, reestablish the place of the African-American man stolen generations ago. We must train the fathers of tomorrow to be the spiritual leaders of their homes, as God intended for them to be.

NOTE

1. "The Willie Lynch Letter: The Making of a Slave!", accessed July 18, 2011, http://www.itsabouttimebpp.com/BPP_Books/pdf/The_Willie_Lynch_Letter_The_Making_Of_A_Slave!.pdf.

PART 2

THE PRODIGAL

FILLING THE VOID

To understand why they are sucked in, recognize the vacuum.

By age fifteen I was pretty much running my own life. I lived at home, but didn't follow any rules except for the ones I made up. I drank heavily, slept with as many women as possible, and came home when I felt like it. I was "that guy" at least in my eyes.

I was a skilled martial artist, wrestler, and dancer. I spent lots of time at the Pride Boxing Gym with boxing greats Mathis, Sr., Mayweather, Sr., and Golden Gloves winner Bryan "The Giant Killer" Blakely. I loved the environment, though I was never a great boxer. I'd suit up and get the snot (quite literally) beaten out of me.

I also danced in a popular group called the All-Star Dancers. We were kids, mostly ages fifteen to seventeen, and I was the youngest. We were committed to dancing and entertainment like no one I had ever seen. We practiced for hours each afternoon. Dancing brought me my greatest joy during those turbulent years of drinking, womanizing, and defiance.

EXTREMES

We took dancing to the next level. People stopped what they were doing to watch the All-Stars whether on stage or a street corner. We created full stage shows complete with smoke and extravagant intros. We were so good that eventually we were not allowed to participate in local dance competitions. We could attend only as special guests.

> People stopped what they were doing to watch the All-Stars whether on stage or a street corner. We created full stage shows complete with smoke and extravagant intros.

Our team captain, B-Mack (my old friend Bill), made sure we stayed away from the ends of the stages because if we came close, the ladies—young and old—would try to pull us off. It got so bad that our manager demanded we not hang around after competitions or events. When we walked outside, lines of people waited to talk to us or have a picture taken with us.

B-Mack, Kareem, Baby D, CraigyQ, and I were the crew to beat. B-Mack always played the role of rapper and dancer MC Hammer. I wore custom-made (by my aunt Jackie Mayweather) harem pants made popular by Hammer. They were baggy at the top and fitted from the knee to the ankle, with side flaps at the hips that buttoned at the waist. Well before television shows such as *America's Got Talent* and *America's Best Dance Crew*, we were taking dancing to the extreme.

We incorporated dance, acrobatics, martial arts, costumes, and even cheap magic tricks. For one routine, we dressed in Zorro hats, black Hammer pants, and black tuxedo shirts. We topped off our costumes with purple and black stonewashed trench coats and our initials cut into the back of our hair.

The announcer yelled, "The All-Star Dancers!" and the crowd went wild. We didn't appear right away, letting the crowd and the music settle down. Everyone expected us to come out with an explosive intro, and we didn't disappoint. All eyes were fixed on the stage as the popular song

"Spend the Night" by the Isley Brothers came on. The crowd went to the next level of crazy, but we still waited.

Then, from the back of the auditorium, we walked down the aisle with our hats banged deep to the left and candles in our hands. We timed everything perfectly. As we arrived onstage, we threw our coats, one at a time, into the crowd at the exact moment we lit "magic" flammable paper and threw it into air. The crowd was in a frenzy! And that was just our four-minute intro.

You can see why we weren't allowed into the competitions, but our dance itch had to be scratched. We were thrilled when the nightclub Pazazz invited us to dance. This was an adult establishment, but we were all fifteen- to seventeen-year-olds! We danced at the club, but also at after events such as women's birthday parties. After awhile, all the major nightclubs booked us, put our name on the marquees, and circulated fliers to draw a crowd. All the success was a strange feeling for me. I was so full of pride knowing that adults—ladies especially—were entertained by my ability to move my body, yet I occasionally felt like a sheep among savage wolves.

> All the success was a strange feeling for me. I was so full of pride knowing that adults—ladies especially—were entertained by my ability to move my body, yet I occasionally felt like a sheep among savage wolves.

EMANCIPATION

My home life deteriorated quickly to say the least. My late hours and rotten behavior weren't cutting it with my mom and dad.

"I'm not going to go through this with you anymore," Dad said. "You need to respect the rules of the house."

"I think it's time for me to go," I responded.

I headed upstairs to pack my things and spend my last night in my childhood home. I woke up after a brief sleep and spent most of the night contemplating this very difficult and life-altering decision. I had concluded that it wasn't in my best interest to leave, but my selfishness won out. I wanted my freedom and was intrigued with the idea of doing my own thing, being my own boss. Deep down, I knew something was wrong with the picture of freedom I'd painted in my head, but my pride would not allow me to withdraw my statement that it was time for me to leave.

My mom and dad were waiting for me in the living room when I got up. I told them of my plan to move in with B-Mack, who lived with a family who had moved here from Chicago. He was all of seventeen and captain of the All-Star Dancers. My parents talked with B-Mack to verify that I had a place to sleep, then said their good-byes.

I drove away from that house emotionally crushed and mentally bewildered. I wanted to stand on my own and despised the rules of my parents. But at the same time I felt like something had just been ripped from my chest.

> I wanted to stand on my own and despised the rules of my parents. But at the same time I felt like something had just been ripped from my chest.

I moved in with B-Mack and the McKinney family on the southeast side of Grand Rapids. We lived on Woodlawn Street, right in the middle of the hood where all the action was taking place. Naomi and Sharif McKinney were some of the most giving people, but this loving family had deep roots in gang activity in Chicago. They welcomed me, fed and clothed me, and accepted me with no questions asked. Despite my hang-ups and imperfections, I felt accepted, embraced, and respected. They became my surrogate family, but they and B-Mack were heavy into the street life. He taught me more about women and drinking and all he thought I needed to know to be a success on the cold, riotous streets.

By sixteen I was drinking heavily, pouring down my throat anything that was placed in front of me. The only time I was even close to sober was when I practiced with the All-Star Dancers. I was a promiscuous, alcoholic kid drowning in pride, looking for love in every wrong place and with all kinds of wrong people. In my drunken stupor, I was oblivious to the emotional turmoil I caused myself and those I loved.

Surprisingly, I concluded that my desire to be accepted and embraced could not be fulfilled through women or alcohol. This inability to satisfy my yearnings was frustrating and continued to reap unfruitful results. The aspiration to be loved created a seemingly unquenchable thirst, and started me on my destructive journey that nearly ended in disaster.

SEEING THE NEED

Those who work with youth and adults in an urban context must take into account that many foundational needs are unmet, leaving no launching pad for a successful life. Youth workers, pastors, lay leaders, and others can find help in paying close attention to the lower levels of Maslow's Hierarchy of Needs and the Search Institute's Forty Developmental Assets for Adolescents.

Abraham Maslow introduced his ideas for the hierarchy of needs in 1943, first in a research paper and then in a book. He suggested that if the most basic human needs are not met (those on the bottom of his pyramid of needs), it is extremely difficult for a person to reach the highest level of the pyramid. The needs are divided into five levels.

1. Physiological Needs. These are basic needs vital to survival, such as water, food, air, and sleep. When these needs go unmet, no other needs can follow.
2. Security Needs. These are safety and security and include a desire for steady employment, health care, safe neighborhoods, and adequate shelter.

3. Social Needs. These needs are for belonging, love, and affection. Relationships—friends, family, romantic partners—can meet these needs, as can social and religious groups.

4. Esteem Needs. These include things such as self-esteem, personal worth, social recognition, and accomplishments.

5. Self-Actualizing Needs. This is the highest level on the pyramid. A self-actualized person is self-aware, interested in personal growth and fulfilling his or her potential and less concerned about the opinions of others.

It's easy to see how life in a gritty, poverty-ridden, sexualized, and violent urban culture can thwart personal growth. Struggling every day for food, good housing, a decent job, and a safe neighborhood puts a damper on self-esteem and meeting one's potential. Yet urban ministries seem to focus on those needs higher on the pyramid. If we assume everyone has their foundational needs met, we will address needs they don't have or understand.

The Search Institute is an independent, nonprofit organization committed to providing leadership, knowledge, and resources to promote healthy children, youth, and communities (www.search-institute.org). The group does research and evaluation, provides resources, and builds partnerships to help develop healthy children and adolescents.

> Struggling every day for food and good housing, a decent job and a safe neighborhood puts a damper on self-esteem and meeting one's potential.

They came up with forty building blocks called "developmental assets" that help kids grow up healthy. The list for adolescents (ages twelve through eighteen) is divided into external assets (support, empowerment, boundaries and expectations, constructive use of time) and internal assets (commitment to learning, positive values, social competencies, and positive identity).

Understanding these needs can be a useful tool in working with and helping adolescents.

Jesus understood the reality of seeing into the basic needs of people. He said in Matthew 25:34–40:

Then the King will say to those on the right, "Come, you who are blessed by my Father, inherit the Kingdom prepared for you from the creation of the world. For I was hungry, and you fed me. I was thirsty, and you gave me a drink. I was a stranger, and you invited me into your home. I was naked, and you gave me clothing. I was sick, and you cared for me. I was in prison, and you visited me." Then these righteous ones will reply, "Lord, when did we ever see you hungry and feed you? Or thirsty and give you something to drink? Or a stranger and show you hospitality? Or naked and give you clothing? When did we ever see you sick or in prison and visit you?" And the King will say, "I tell you the truth, when you did it to one of the least of these my brothers and sisters, you were doing it to me!" (NLT)

TAKE IT HOME

The body of Christ can do any number of practical things to help those around us, the most important being to build relationships. When we build relationships, we build a family. And within a family, few needs go unmet. If your child is hungry, the family doesn't think twice about feeding him. If your child needs a place to stay, the family will empty its bank account to make sure she is safe. In many cases in urban ministry, the ministry becomes the parent or family the "child" needs.

The bottom line is learning to love our neighbors as ourselves. We build relationships of trust, and we see about the needs of the community because they are our neighbors and not people merely receiving a handout.

I don't argue that receiving such gifts can engender an attitude of entitlement, but as we build authentic relationships, the entitlement disappears in the firm embrace of family and trust. The real question for the church is: Are we willing to build authentic relationships?

7

STREET WISE

False teachers will rush in where mentors fear to tread.

My promiscuous lifestyle caught up with me. At age sixteen, I learned that I would soon be a father. The news was devastating because I knew I wasn't fit to care for myself, much less a child. Yet knowing I would have a child of my own triggered a sense of pride and joy.

My child's mother and I met at a grungy teen spot called Maxine's when I was thirteen and she maybe a year older. I was there dancing (as usual); she and her cousins made a bet to see who could get my phone number first. She won. She and I saw each other off and on for several years. Our dates became easier when she and her family moved down the street from my mom's house.

I was involved in her life during the pregnancy despite her playing games with me about who the father of her baby actually was. I was indeed the father, but there were times her words caused me to doubt. Despite the games, I got a call when she went into labor and was able to spend time at the hospital with her. However, her mom kicked me out as the birth neared. Still, I got to hold my son, Anthony Tarell Williams, soon after he was born on January 1, 1989. I was sixteen, his mother just seventeen. I decided to give him my middle name (Anthony) because until then I didn't know if he was my child. But after I held him in my arms, I was convinced that this was my little man.

Anthony and his mother moved in with me (and B-Mack) for five months. Together we cared for the newborn, feeding and diapering him, sitting up with him at night. But that 120-pound girl was a serious brawler. She would fight both boys and girls, and when she got angry she'd turn on me. Despite my training and background, I never hit her. I'd sit and take the blows and do nothing because I could not see myself ever hitting a woman. I would hold her and tell her to stop, but when I let her go she'd come at me and scratch my neck. Rarely during those months after Anthony's birth did I not have claw marks on my neck. But one day I stood up to her and told her this had gone on too long. If she touched me again, I would seriously hurt her. Soon after that, we decided that we should not be together.

> It was easy for B-Mack and me to become involved in the gang thanks to where we lived and our close social contact with the General, Poopie's brother-in-law and B-Mack's uncle.

As Anthony grew older, his mother and I would care for him a month at a time, she returning to her family and me caring for the baby. She'd come get him for a little while, then bring him back to me. I was a single father off and on for months. But I had help raising my boy thanks to Naomi (nicknamed Poopie) McKinney. My son still calls Naomi "Na-Na."

It was easy for B-Mack and me to become involved in the gang thanks to where we lived and our close social contact with the General, Poopie's brother-in-law and B-Mack's uncle. The General reported to Poopie's brother, who lived in Chicago.

As we partied our way through the days and nights, the house grew worse for the wear. That's when Naomi sent over Granny, her mom, to live with us. She kept the house clean and made our meals, but this was no typical granny.

This granny was off the hook! She always wore a red rag on her head and seemed to always have a cigarette hanging from her lips. She provided the sound system and music for all of our parties and always carried a pistol on her. We hid our own weapons because Granny loved to find and study each of our guns. One time she took B-Mack's sawed-off rifle and claimed it as her own.

LOOKING FOR MENTORS IN ALL THE WRONG PLACES

I had several street mentors during these years. First was B-Mack, just a year or two older than me. He was nephew of the General of the gang, who we also called Low Down. B-Mack knew more about the streets than I did. He taught me what I needed to know about the block where we lived, selling dope, drinking, and women; I looked up to him as a mentor and friend. We got into a good number of scrapes together, always looking out for each other's backs. B-Mack showed his love for me by teaching me what he knew. But we were both kids trying to put on the clothing of the street life we wanted to live and own.

> The General . . . had a weird value system: working every day to provide for his wife and child, but also running the Grand Rapids chapter of a big Chicago gang.

Another mentor was the General. Poopie had moved to Grand Rapids to get away from her past life and the mean streets of Chicago. The General and his wife, Poopie's sister, soon moved as well and brought a strange division into the lives of those around them.

The General counseled B-Mack and me to stay away from gang life; he told me to stay in school and care for my son. He had a weird value system: working every day to provide for his wife and child, but also running the Grand Rapids chapter of a big Chicago gang. I was one of the few people allowed into his inner circle. I was permitted to visit his home; we went to the movies, and even played catch in his yard sometimes in the middle of the night. He offered me advice and a listening ear, and I valued the opinions and good relationship with this older man.

> To me, being part of a gang was a way to have both power and family at least the way the General modeled life for me.

But the gang life was so embedded in his blood (there are now five generations of gang members in the family) that he couldn't do anything differently. The General had a glimpse of hope for us, however, and urged us to get out, though he couldn't and wouldn't himself. I wanted to be like Low Down, a general who was respected on the streets yet who loved and took care of his family.

STREET SMART

I remember watching the General in action at a huge concert where the All-Star Dancers were special guests. We danced in our red and black outfits, gang symbols cut into our hair. Suddenly a fellow gang member walked in the room and opened fire with a machine gun. I saw the General walk up alongside this cat and say to him, "Tommy, we're here to dance, so put that gun away and let's go home." And Tommy did it! I didn't think such a thing was possible. That was power, I thought, and I wanted it. To me, being part of a gang was a way to have both power and family at least the way the General modeled life for me.

I made my living in my mid-teen years by living off the land. I hustled, took odd jobs, and learned to cut hair. With her sisters, my aunt Diane owned and ran a hair salon named PJ's after my grandfather. I'd cut hair at the salon, as well as on the street corners and porches. I was pretty good because I could draw too. I'd draw a picture or someone's initials, then cut it into the back of that person's hair.

I met Too Short when I started cutting his hair. Too Short introduced me to Below Zero, a local drug dealer who liked my hair-cutting techniques. Below Zero flashed money around, paying me fifty dollars and a backpack full of liquor or clothes for one haircut. Money and liquor: the siren call was too much for me to ignore. I got my first dope sack from Too Short. The plan was to cut up the dope and sell it in smaller pieces for profit.

The plan worked! We made a little money and went back for more, spending our profits on liquor and clothes. But our money-making venture was on precarious footing.

One night B-Mack and I cruised the city in a car we'd rented for the night from an addict (we called cars like that a rent-a-base). We drove much of the night, looking to sell the drugs we'd hidden. We stayed up most of the night, then started roaming the streets again in the morning.

In retrospect, it was no surprise B-Mack and I were pulled over by the police. They asked us to step out of the car and we were sure we'd get busted. B-Mack had his drugs hidden in his hat, which of course they found. I had hidden my drugs in my underwear, but I wore two pair of regular shorts. My outer shorts fell to the ground as the officer searched me, but the officers didn't check any further.

> In retrospect, it was no surprise B-Mack and I were pulled over by the police. They asked us to step out of the car and we were sure we'd get busted.

I was sent home, while B-Mack was loaded into the squad car and taken downtown to the police station. I remember the long walk home to tell the family—the General, Poopie, and Sharif—that B-Mack was in jail for selling drugs. I don't think they knew we were selling.

THE HARD WAY

I sat, trembling, in my room at the Woodlawn house awaiting a visit from the General. I couldn't find the words to explain. He gave me the third degree; I don't believe I've ever heard the word *stupid* used so many times in the same conversation before or since. I told him who gave us the package of drugs, and the General suggested I roll with him over to this big-time dealer's house (I think he was being sarcastic).

So maybe we owed one thousand dollars to Too Short, and maybe we had spent some already on clothes and the car rental and had lost the drugs B-Mack was arrested with. But I still had about eight hundred dollars worth of drugs on me. The General insisted that Too Short would get no profit from our little fiasco, so I wasn't expecting the meet between the General and Too Short to go well at all.

The General told me to move away from Too Short's door as he knocked, lowering himself into a fighting stance. Too Short came to the door.

"Did you give this to my nephews?" the General demanded, holding out my sack of unfound drugs.

Too Short swallowed hard, gathering up his words.

"Yep," was all he could come up with.

The General thrust the drugs at him and told him in his I-mean-business-and-you-better-know-that voice that he was never to give us drugs again, that he would need to pay B-Mack's bail, and that Too Short had better stay out of his way.

He did, but Below Zero knew a future dealer when he saw one. Below Zero, introduced to us through Too Short, contacted me and offered to teach me how to sell drugs the right way. Despite the General's disapproval of his nephews selling drugs, I officially set up the business thanks to Below Zero.

Below Zero shared our interest in making money, spending money, and using drugs to finance our lifestyles. He came alongside us to teach us how to buy one rock, divide it, and make a profit. He taught us how to tell an undercover cop from a real buyer and how to avoid a potential bad deal. We learned to hide our drugs well, to get money owed us from our clients, and to pass around our profits when necessary.

> We learned to hide our drugs well, to get money owed us from our clients, and to pass around our profits when necessary.

Ours was a mentoring relationship based on shared interest—illegal, highly danger-ous, addicting, end-up-in-jail interests, but something we shared together that bonded us forever as brothers.

MENTOR GAP

I had three kinds of mentors in my life:

1. Peer to Peer. B-Mack taught me what he knew about living on the streets. We were around the same age and were into the same things. I valued B-Mack for his friendship and the time he took to teach me what he knew.

2. Older to Younger. The General was an older man who took me under his wing, talked to me, set an example for me on how to live with respect. He had a family I admired and who accepted me as their own. The General called me his nephew, though we weren't related by blood at all. I looked up to him as a father figure, especially as I began to parent my own child.

3. Shared Interest. Below Zero and I shared an interest in selling drugs. He taught me everything he knew, and I in turn passed on that knowledge to others. I valued Below Zero's knowledge and his interest in my life regardless of the motivation.

The church offered no mentors to step into my life. I wonder how my life would have been different had my grandfather mentored me instead of the General, if a local older dancer or rapper had stepped in to guide me in my career choice instead of Below Zero, if a teenager from the church youth group had come alongside me to teach me integrity and honesty instead of B-Mack teaching me about the streets.

As pastor of The EDGE, a hip-hop church reaching into the urban culture, I can look back and see that the church missed some real opportunities in my life. I'd grown up going to church, but when it came time to ask for help, drug dealers and gang leaders were there for me, not elders, youth workers, and pastors.

> I wonder how my life would have been different had my grandfather mentored me instead of the General, if a local older dancer or rapper had stepped in to guide me in my career choice instead of Below Zero, if a teenager from the church youth group had come alongside me to teach me integrity and honesty instead of B-Mack teaching me about the streets.

We, the church, must fill in the gaps in the lives of youth and young adults. If we don't do it, somebody else will. If we're not available, young people will find an open ear and heart out on the streets. If we're arguing about small, churchy things, the gangs will be happy to fill our kids' minds with new, seemingly better, more exciting ways to live.

Jason Holdridge, lead pastor of Impact Church in Lowell, Michigan, preached a message about the family that I remember well. His premise was that "our families do not have exciting stories." He said that the streets will grab our kids because the streets give them something to live for. But families, not the streets, must be the ones to give our kids a reason to live.

Ministries must become a beachhead for the war-torn young people who roam the streets of our urban centers: the body of Christ, willing helpers to ease their sorrows and heal their souls. If our doors aren't open, somebody else's will be. If the ministries do not provide opportunities for exploration, the dude on the street will.

TAKE IT HOME

Here are several tips for building a mentorship culture within your ministry:

1. Most importantly, the leader must believe it, buy into it, and live it out. Mentorship is a ministry-wide investment into our communities, so the leader must be able to cast his vision from a personal place.

2. The youth worker must know that youth ministry as usual is not going to work in the urban context. The kids may have fun at an event and want to come back, but the ministry can't be interested in simply creating fun times. Teens do not need a teenage daycare center or a Sunday pizza night with wild games. They need adults to intentionally pour into them; they need a community of believers committed to making disciples in unique and exciting ways.

3. Help all volunteers understand the reality of the community and the need for proactive movement. They must know and understand that if ministries aren't providing intentional mentorship, the streets will.

4. Provide mentorship education for staff and volunteers. I recommend *Coaching 101: Discover the Power of Coaching* by Robert E. Logan, Sherilyn Carlton, and Tara Miller, though there are other books and guides available.

5. Encourage a culture of healthy mentoring through a four-way program:

   - Older to Younger—Encourage both the younger people and the older members of your church to get to know one another. Help the older to pour into the younger.

- Peer to Peer—Encourage accountability among peers; partner more rooted believers with newer ones.
- Shared Interest—Find out a young person's interests and match them with an older believer who can show them how to operate in their area of passion in a God-honoring way.
- Pour into Others—Encourage young people to find someone else they can pour into. This encourages the next generation of mentors.

6. Just do it! Whether you have one or one thousand volunteers, just get started. Mentoring only takes one to begin reaching out.

8

THE GANG WAY

The draw of even a destructive community is love, acceptance, and meaning.

My conversion to the gang world was complete by the time I was seventeen. Like many others who join a gang, I had several opportunities to say no to street life. But strange acts of kindness—like the General helping B-Mack and me with the drug issue and his accepting me into his family—drew me in. I chose to move full throttle into the street life, and it cost me dearly.

I felt like the gang made me part of something bigger than myself, something with colors and symbols that were nationally recognized. I became part of a peer group and family that stretched across the nation, so in my eyes the "love" I could receive from the gang was endless. Everyone in my life up until then—adults, church, school—insisted that I change who I was to fit in. The gang, however, saw my unproductive and useless lifestyle and embraced and cultivated it.

Now I was accepted for drinking, selling drugs, dropping out of school, sleeping with women, and avoiding all manner of productive work. Not a bad gig for a seventh-grade dropout! I remember thinking that I was finally around "normal" people simply because their behavior patterns were similar to my own, and they accepted me for who I was.

THE BROTHERHOOD

The gang—part of a national organization that I have chosen not to name—had weekly meetings that were as structured as any corporate meeting I have ever attended. We met at 5:55 p.m. on Fridays, the fifth day of the week. It was a strange division: a gang dedicated to so much activity against the law would stop at each meeting to pray facing the east. We adopted and adapted some of the principles of Islam and the Moorish Orthodox Catechism, praying something like, "Allah, Father of the universe, Father of love, truth, peace, freedom, and justice . . . Allah is my guide and protector by night and by day, through your holy prophet, Noble Drew Ali . . . all is well."

Meetings were attended by gang members from several neighborhoods, all of whom were involved in a variety of illegal activities such as selling dope or guns or running prostitution houses. Each meeting included taking minutes, updates on what was going on in each set (neighborhood), and suggestions for how we could resolve any "issues."

> It was a strange division: a gang dedicated to so much activity against the law would stop at each meeting to pray facing the east. We adopted and adapted some of the principles of Islam and the Moorish Orthodox Catechism.

One example is the time we had a beef with another crew and needed to discuss the details of how we would respond to these guys. They had shot up a neighborhood where a group of our guys were. No one was hurt, but we were embarrassed. We developed a response strategy and moved out accordingly. Another meeting ended with a shoot-out, thanks to a visiting gang that drove by and opened fire. We dove for cover, but the more experienced gang members pulled out their weapons and began firing back. The rivals made the mistake of yelling their gang name as they drove by; retribution on our part would soon be coming.

The General would pass the hat to collect dues, which would then be used to finance the rest of the evening's festivities. We met at the house on Woodlawn Street or in the nearby projects, and Granny would cut up and fry a chicken or two, along with fish, and set out a variety of other foods. Sometimes a hundred people (gang members, friends, women) would attend. We passed the drink and smoke around, only to the left, for those who chose to partake.

As the evening progressed, the General would sit us down and tell war stories about our "brothers" in the gang before us, regaling us with tales of evading the law, making big money selling dope, or fighting and defeating rival gangs. Current members would play basketball, wrestle, or "bust some spades" on a card table set up in the living room or on the porch. These meetings felt so much like the family gatherings of my youth when everyone gathered at my uncle Sonny's house next door to my mom's.

One rite of passage was my first journey to Chicago, the mecca for the gang. This huge meeting was hosted by a gang officer who lived in Chicago. The trip was an ordeal for me, first because I'd grown up in the much smaller city of Grand Rapids; second because I felt I needed to prove myself worthy of gang membership.

We learned that we had been keeping much of the original intent and traditions of the gang in place, which was great for all who attended. But to see a park full of

> The love I felt in Chicago fortified the foundation of my personal commitment to both the local and national organization.

people who walked, talked, stood, and dressed like me left a lasting impression on my heart. This was confirmation that the lessons we'd learned in our hometown were based on "true love" for one another and the gang. The love I felt in Chicago fortified the foundation of my personal commitment to both the local and national organization. We were not treated as if we were poor cousins of this great gang, but instead we were encouraged to study our lit (rules of engagement), listen to the General, and continue the "good fight."

I was awarded the honor of taking gang writings from the 1970s handed down from the fathers of the gang and distributing them throughout Grand Rapids. I took my time drawing a cover for the booklet, feeling it a great honor to have been selected to transcribe what Grand Rapids would come to know as the lit, a document that dictates the behavior of our gang. This project marked me as an up-and-coming gang leader, a path I relished.

BLOOD LUST

I also relished a little blood-letting, which happened soon enough.

That cool, springtime night was like so many others. I was hanging with my boys at the house on Woodlawn Street. We were hungry, so we headed down to Cutie Pie's for beer and snacks at eleven o'clock. A walk to Cutie Pie's meant smelling that smoky barbeque, sniffing the hazy air, and almost tasting the smoked ribs and Polish sausage—we called them Cutie Dogs—always on the grill.

Five of us, including the General, ambled down the street, full of ourselves and wired up from the Christian Brothers brandy and Miller High Life we'd just finished guzzling. We didn't anticipate trouble, but a dude got too close. The General didn't like people getting too close, especially if we didn't know them. But this guy wouldn't stop. He kept walking toward the General, despite our telling him to step back.

The General swung his head side to side, measuring each of us for the task at hand. We all wondered what would happen, eager to please yet cautious about stepping out of line.

"Bat, take care of this dude."

Bat was me.

I never hesitated. I kicked that offending dude in the side, then kicked him in the head. The guy went down in a hurry.

He was still down when we came back out of the store.

The adrenaline rush was better than getting drunk. I'd been questioning whether I'd be up for the challenge when the General called me out, but now I knew the answer. "I can do this!" I crowed to myself.

It was my first taste of blood, and I took ownership. I knew I could do great bodily harm, and that knowledge felt great. My guys were just as amped. I'd been a park legend, somebody they'd heard about who could put it down. But until that night, they'd not seen me in action. They jabbered, swore, and laughed, pumping me up with their own excitement. I was the man that night, a tough kid who could beat another and not flinch—a young man who refined a taste for violence in a moment that would direct his life for years to come. I turned toward violence, embraced it, and never looked back.

> It was first taste of blood, and I took ownership. I knew that I could do great bodily harm, and that knowledge felt great.

I did look down, however, when my foot felt strange. I'd kicked that man so hard that the metal tip on my Bobby Brown shoes bent nearly double.

I didn't care. I'd drawn blood and won. I was on the mountaintop.

SIGNS OF LOVE

At the beginning of my gang involvement, I was living a double life. I was still involved with the All-Star Dancers when our group caught the eye of the 4-H Club. They believed in us, so much so that they opened a dance school for us to run. I can still see the freshly painted purple walls and dancer silhouettes painted over top. Eight-foot mirrors lined the walls. The space seemed like a dream come true for us.

The General heard about the dance school and came over to check it out. He also came over to give us another opportunity to get out of the gang. He told us we had a chance to become something other than a banger, but B-Mack and I decided we could live double lives. We were dancers by day and hoodlums by night.

It didn't take long before my reputation as a banger and drug dealer eclipsed my reputation as a dancer. Back in the day, people from the worst of the hood considered drug dealers to be lower than low—truly horrible people. The 4-H Club heard from the community that B-Mack and I had another life and threw us out of "our" studio so fast it was crazy. We acted like it didn't faze us—we were All-Stars and bangers!— but the reality is that it crushed us. Dancing was one thing we were best at, and we blew it.

> It didn't take long before my reputation as a banger and drug dealer eclipsed my reputation as a dancer.

I almost blew it with Gotti, a young man higher up in the gang than me. He had moved to Grand Rapids from Chicago when he was thirteen. By age fourteen, he was six feet tall and about 200 pounds of muscle. He quickly gained the respect of most people in the organization. He and I, on the other hand, never saw eye to eye, metaphorically or literally. I was five feet seven and 140 pounds soaking wet and with bricks in my pocket. It seemed like every time the gang gathered, he would pick at me until I was ready to fight. We'd go at it until we were tired or another member broke us up, just about guaranteeing we'd get a rule violation.

This cycle went on for about two years until one night he picked a fight again. But this time I picked back. We fought, and from that night on were as close as blood brothers. We were committed to each other even unto death. All he had to do was say the word and I would do whatever he needed, and he the same for me.

I spoke to both Gotti, former leader of the gang, and his brother B-Mack before writing this book and sharing these stories; they gave me their blessings. But Gotti also outlined his reasons for staying with the gang: "I am down with this for life. I have given all that I have into this, and I will not let it go."

He went on to say that the General (his uncle) showed him nothing but love and how to be a man, and that he and all of us gang members were all he had. He talked to me about several things I had done for him. One was soon after he arrived in Grand Rapids. He had been kicked out of his aunt's house and, at age fifteen, had no place to stay and no money. I sat outside with him and his limited luggage on her porch in the rain. I had nothing to offer him except a drink, conversation, and compassion.

> To Gotti, these were signs of love of the highest order as fellow gang members. More than isolated acts of kindness, he saw me as an ambassador of the organization and attributed my actions to the gang we both served.

He also remembered a time he had planned to fight after school. The kid he was to fight called in his older brother and friends, who vowed to wait for Gotti at the bus stop. Gotti called the Woodlawn Street house and I answered. I told him I'd wait at the bus stop to help him. The other guys knew me and didn't want to start a beef, so the fight never happened.

To Gotti, these were signs of love of the highest order as fellow gang members. More than isolated acts of kindness, he saw me as an ambassador of the organization and attributed my actions to the gang we both served.

I, too, have incidents that meant everything to me, including peers and old-school gang members from Chicago willing to share stories from the past and talk to us about the "rules" of the game. This meant so much because time spent with an older person and personal attention from women were ultimate expressions of love to many gang members. Though the ramifications of being in a gang are devastating, involvement has a sweet smell to a desperate heart yearning to be loved.

TAKE IT HOME

Gang talk, ranks, and principles (love, truth, peace, freedom, justice) are full of military, as well as spiritual, allusions. The military often uses terms such as *freedom*, *peace*, and *justice*. Many forms of spiritual practice talk of love, truth, and peace. From Buddhism to Islam, Bushido to Judaism, the principles we taught in the gangs mirrored those taught in religions around the world. Our practices, however, were a world away from those of law-abiding, peace-loving, spiritual people.

As Christian churches work in the urban culture, it's instructive to know how the two compare. Take a look at what love, truth, peace, freedom, and justice look like from a gang perspective, and how the Bible offers a different view.

Love

Gang. The gang is capable of providing only a temporary, surface love based on what you are able to do for me. How you show love is contingent on your environment. The reality is that all the world has to offer is destruction.

The Bible. Matthew 22:36–40: "'Teacher, which is the greatest commandment in the Law?' Jesus replied: 'Love the Lord your God with all your heart and with all your soul and with all your mind.' This is the first and greatest commandment. And the second is like it: 'Love your neighbor as yourself.' All the Law and the Prophets hang on these two commandments."

Truth

Gang. The gang world has its truth. However, the truth of street life is not rooted in anything sustainable. Rather, it is rooted in hatred and a misuse of hearts committed to a shallow cause.

The Bible. John 14:6: "Jesus answered, 'I am the way and the truth and the life. No one comes to the Father except through me.'"

Peace

Gang. Peace in the street life is nonexistent. It's the ultimate oxymoron.

The Bible. Psalm 29:10–11: "The LORD sits enthroned over the flood; the LORD is enthroned as King forever. The LORD gives strength to his people; the LORD blesses his people with peace."

Freedom

Gang. At first the street life screams, "FREEEEEEDOM at last!" We tried to sell young people on the idea that they would no longer have to live according to the rules of "the man" (whoever that was), who wanted to hold them back. The truth of the matter is that gang members are strapped down, subject to the invisible chains of the organization and the consequences of their actions.

The Bible. Galatians 5:13: "You, my brothers [and sisters], were called to be free. But do not use your freedom to indulge the sinful nature; rather, serve one another in love."

Justice

Gang. The bottom line was justice, we thought. I lived and breathed "Justice is mine," saith Troy. Taking situations into our own hands convinced us that we were in some way getting justice.

The Bible. Isaiah 42:2–4: "He will not shout or cry out, or raise his voice in the streets. A bruised reed he will not break, and a smoldering wick he will not snuff out. In faithfulness he will bring forth justice; he will not falter or be discouraged till he establishes justice on earth. In his law the islands will put their hope."

9

GANG FAMILY VALUES

Teaching values requires learning what they value.

A year of living on my own had turned me into a different person. It seemed like overnight my mind was transformed; I started to become numb to the harsh reality of street life. My life was consumed with "earning" and giving respect in the streets I wanted to own.

I quickly became an officer in the gang organization, moving up the leadership ladder during my late teens. Great responsibility was placed on my shoulders as ambassador of the gang. This was an honor, but an enormous amount of baggage accompanied a leadership role. I was once the life of every party I visited, using my dancing to dazzle the crowd. But as a gang leader, I was stopped at the door every time, searched, and asked not to start any trouble.

My attitude toward my family and neighborhood changed too. One night as I rode in a taxi down Francis Street where I had spent by childhood, I saw my older brother Mark, our cousin Mike, and his brother Butch. I had the driver do a U-turn, then jumped out of the car. My brother was drinking, something I had never seen him do. He was a square in my eyes, never doing anything wrong and always working out.

I told them to jump in the car, flashed some cash at them, and bought them all the alcohol they wanted. We visited a party at a fellow gang member's house; they were impressed by all the girls, drugs, and feeling of brotherhood. When I dropped them off back on Francis Street, I didn't feel nostalgia for my old haunts or warmth for my family. I felt greed, pride, and ownership. I decided right then to take over Francis Street.

> Respect is an unspoken rule that the street life takes very seriously. The name of the game is to gain respect and dish it out as fast as you get it.

I told the General about my plan to take over Francis Street one day, and started visiting my family to prep them for what might happen.

RESPECT

Respect is an unspoken rule that the street life takes very seriously. The name of the game is to gain respect and dish it out as fast as you get it. The gang also had rules regarding behavior and respect, which created a complex layering of codes of behavior that gang members were meticulous about following.

We could get a violation for fighting with a fellow gang member, dating two female members at the same time, and disrespecting a fellow member. Punishment was quick and harsh. I was often put "on the wall" as punishment, meaning the biggest, strongest gang members hit me in the chest fifty-five times. If your crime was big enough, you could catch the beat-down of your life. In extreme cases, even worse happened.

Everything we did was about gaining the respect of rival gangs. Violence against rival gangs was usually about them disrespecting us in some way such as threatening one of us, selling drugs on our turf, or using violence against one of our members. More than a few times, the beef was started because of a girl. It was like clockwork: if one of the sistas went out to a club, we were almost guaranteed trouble that night. Often guys from the other gangs would try to kick it with one or a group of girls in our gang.

Either the girl would feel disrespected or the dude's girlfriend would have something to say. Either way, it was a recipe for a bar brawl. We would arrive to clean up the mess, and I'm not talking sweeping up the glass or broken chairs.

For me, respect was where it was at. Everything I did was about gaining and keeping respect. Every conversation hinged on respect; every action was studied under the lens of respect; every transaction had to be layered with respect.

Our code of honor was strict, but my own was even more so. I lived by the law that you never turn your back on family or the people in your gang. My way of thinking was dominated by that one word: *respect*. You always respect your family and the nation (the gang), and you do whatever it takes to keep that in people's minds. One day I heard of a young brother disrespecting his mother. He'd called her a foul name and hollered at her. This was out of line in my book.

> Our code of honor was strict, but my own was even more so. I lived by the law that you never turn your back on family or the people in your gang.

Several of us were sitting on my uncle Sonny's porch getting juiced on liquor. That young brother sat with us as if nothing had happened. I had talked with him earlier on the phone, telling him I was going to get at him. That day I could wait no longer. I jumped out of my seat and dragged him down the stairs. I hauled him around the house and threw him onto the hood of my car.

I jammed my pistol into his mouth.

"Do you think I care about life at all? Respect is everything to me," I said, anger grinding my words into his ears and grinding the gun barrel into the back of his mouth.

"If you ever disrespect your mother again, I'll blow your mouth out without a second thought."

He stared at me, his eyes wide and his breathing shallow. He nodded ever so slightly, and I pulled the gun out of his mouth. He slid to the ground as I walked away.

The scariest part? He was my god-brother Kenny. I was so far gone if I could do that to a young man as close to me as any brother can be.

THE CODE

My job as a leader was to enforce the code when necessary as a way of creating our gang culture. I had seen the gang's general enforce the code and had also seen him delegate enforcement to others. Now it was my turn to be the enforcer.

Nobody steals from a brother. I knew this; the General taught it. Everybody knew that you broke the honor code when you stole from a brother. But one of the cats had broken this law, and it was up to me to dispense justice.

> My job as a leader was to enforce the code when necessary as a way of creating our gang culture.

We gathered at the house on Francis Street. I had no trouble calling this brother out over the trouble. Of course he denied having stolen anything—repeatedly denied it.

I took him to the back room of the house. It was me, him, and my .38 revolver. Without a word, I dumped the bullets out of the revolver, then took one and slid it back in. I spun the cylinder, its clicking the only sound in the quiet room. The brother stared at the spinning cylinder, his breathing faster by the second.

"Did you steal from the brother?" I asked.

He denied it.

I pushed that revolver into his knee and pulled the trigger.

Nothing.

"Did you steal from the brother?" I asked again, this time more intensely.

He denied it again, but the sweat broke out on his forehead.

I pulled the trigger again.

Nothing.

"Did you steal from the brother?"

The boy broke into tears in front of me. He wept; tears and snot running down his face. His body shook as he finally admitted that he had indeed stolen from a fellow gang member.

> I've seen friends and enemies shot down in front of me, but nothing prepared me for the pain of knowing my little brother had been shot.

I had gotten the confession and reinforced my status as a gang leader.

That boy served as an example to the brothers of what would happen if the stealing continued. And it was a strong statement. He stayed in the gang, but disappeared completely about a year later.

The street took its toll on me and on my family. My gang involvement brought trouble to those around me, including my younger half-brother, Titus. Titus and his girlfriend had driven up to the hill, an area of Grand Rapids controlled by a rival gang that had vowed to exterminate my gang.

Apparently Titus and his girl were in the wrong place at the wrong time, and the rival gang opened fire on them. Titus lost a couple of fingers and his girlfriend was severely injured. They were rushed to the hospital.

I've seen friends and enemies shot down in front of me, but nothing prepared me for the pain of knowing my little brother had been shot. When I received word that Titus had been hurt, I remember one of the strangest emotions I've ever felt. I was so enraged that I couldn't cry or talk. All I saw was blood, and all I knew was that somebody had to pay for this incident.

Perhaps my feelings of injustice had to do with the fact that Titus had never been involved in the gangs. Perhaps my feelings had to do with knowing that Titus, an athlete with extraordinary basketball skills, had his life changed forever. It was all of that, but it was also feeling like that bullet had belonged to me. I was the gangbanger; I was the one who was involved in violence; I was the one who led a life of crime; I was the one who the rival gang would have loved to kill or injure. Instead, they hurt an innocent boy who had a chance to get off the streets thanks to his athletic skills.

> I have often found that underneath some of the thick shells that exist in this culture, the real person is generally not happy with the lifestyle.

People often ask me how to get gangbangers to step away from the life they say they love so much. Folks want to know how a clean, honest, safe life can be compared to all the money and fame the street life has to offer.

My response is quite simple: It can't. It is not our job to match or guarantee the money and fame the streets offer. What God offers is much greater than riches and fame. What God offers is hope and a future. This is my message to gangbangers.

My first step is to ask them to evaluate what is most important to them, what their core values are. But I don't think I've ever used the words *core values* with a gangbanger. I talk their talk, asking them what they love, what's golden for them. From the most dangerous dudes to the average cat off the block, all have a set of core values. If someone had asked me about such things back in the day, I would have said family was most important.

Once I establish what is important to them, I ask how street life helps them move closer to that. If family is most important, how does running dope help keep their family safe? If safety is important, how do constant threats of violence and carrying a gun guarantee safety? I have often found that underneath some of the thick shells that exist in this culture, the real person is generally not happy with the lifestyle.

I'm not sure how I would have responded if someone had pointed out the possibility of my brothers getting shot due to my violent lifestyle. But at the minimum, it would have gotten my attention which would have opened a small window of opportunity. The small window could have led to offering me the hope and restoration I thought lost to me forever.

This concept can be illustrated by the example of Peter and John blessing the beggar as they made their way to the temple to pray. There are several principles to gain from this encounter that apply to reaching out to gangbangers:

One day Peter and John were going up to the temple at the time of prayer—at three in the afternoon. Now a man crippled from birth was being carried to the temple gate called Beautiful, where he was put every day to beg from those going into the temple courts. When he saw Peter and John about to enter, he asked them for money. Peter looked straight at him, as did John. Then Peter said, "Look at us!" So the man gave them his attention, expecting to get something from them. Then Peter said, "Silver or gold I do not have, but what I have I give you. In the name of Jesus Christ of Nazareth, walk." Taking him by the right hand, he helped him up, and instantly the man's feet and ankles became strong. He jumped to his feet and began to walk. Then he went with them into the temple courts, walking and jumping, and praising God. When all the people saw him walking and praising God, they recognized him as the same man who used to sit begging at the temple gate called Beautiful, and they were filled with wonder and amazement at what had happened to him. (Acts 3:1–10)

TAKE IT HOME

Reaching out to urban youth and gang members is not easy. Try these steps that Peter and John did:

1. Meet Them Where They Are. Just as Peter and John met the beggar at the temple gate, so must we meet gangbangers where they are.

That might mean living in the neighborhood, attending street fairs, visiting their schools and homes, and talking to them on the street corners. Don't expect urban kids to show up at your church; expect to meet them on the streets where they live.

2. Make Promises God Can Keep. Peter and John didn't promise the lame man money or goods. They addressed his physical and spiritual needs. You can't promise gangbangers a richer, more bling-filled life; but you can offer spiritual hope and restoration in God. You can help a banger walk to a new life of peace. You can help the banger see that what you have to offer will help them as it relates to their core values.

3. Come Alongside to Help. The Jesus-followers helped the lame man up, then accompanied him into the temple. They didn't just heal and walk away. Helping urban youth isn't a one-shot deal. It's a long, often difficult commitment to provide help and a safe haven. That can include a good meal, a place to stay, homework help, life skills training, financial training and help, or assistance in dealing with social services agencies. It's living life with the people you meet.

4. Help Them Develop a New Normal. The lame man's normal had been sitting on a mat begging. His new normal was leaping, running, and praising God. A gangbanger who leaves or an urban kid who finds Christ has a new life. The old way of living—with its friends, hangouts, activities—will be gone. Help provide new places to hang out (with purpose), activities, role models, and friends.

5. Trust God for the Results. Peter and John commanded the lame man to get up and walk. He was healed only when he did so. Peter and John trusted that Jesus would provide the healing if they did their part. Every kid you meet isn't going to make a life change with God

in mind. Every person isn't going to like you, want to change, or even care. Fortunately, you're not in charge; God is, so let him do his work while you do what he calls you to do.

10

RESPECT OF THE FALLEN

Redemption begins when we can see the virtue in their honor.

The juxtapositions were bizarre. The guy who fronted me my first drugs, Below Zero, was a firm believer in the Bible. In fact, he would tell me he was a follower of Jesus. But he would also admit that he had issues like everyone else. He had a moral side that made him say it wasn't cool for me to sell drugs. After he figured out my desire, he introduced me to every dope dealer he knew because, I think, he wanted me to see that there was no need for one more dealer.

Below Zero was nice in so many ways. I told him the All-Star Dancers needed a sponsor for a dance we wanted to attend, so he bought shoes for all of us. But what he didn't know was that by sharing his profits with us, showing me all the dope dealers and how they lived, and sharing his knowledge with me, I was being influenced even more by seeing the power these guys had. I thought that if I gained that kind of power and money, I could get myself and my dance group out of Grand Rapids. That didn't happen, but I often dreamed about a new life.

Crazy is the best word to describe my drug-selling days. I never used the stuff, which is a miracle in itself, but I sure knew how to sell it. That first experience started with Below Zero and me sitting in his car drinking Courvoisier. I asked him to show me how to flip dope. He looked at me a minute, then reached into his pocket and gave me a twenty-dollar bill. We headed to Too Short's house, where Below Zero talked to Too Short about my flipping.

> We studied the lights on the police cars and how the engines of Crown Victorias or Grand Marquis (police vehicles of choice) sounded in the night.

Too Short took that twenty and gave me two rocks, about forty dollars' worth of drugs. I stayed at that house for three days learning the game, and I was able to flip that original twenty-dollar bill into six hundred dollars. I was then able to buy my first weight, about a half ounce of cocaine, and cut it how I wanted to. I left that drug tutorial with my life on a new track.

DEALER

I sold drugs either from a house or on a street corner in the Madison Square area of southeast Grand Rapids. I would work that block for days straight, handling the business when others got tired and headed home. But that block was borderline suicide, seeing as we stood there with lots of drugs and just about everyone knew it.

My best friend, CraigyQ, and I stood on that corner in rain, sleet, and snow with the jump-out boys (drug task force) swooping down about monthly. If we were caught with any crack in the late 1980s and early '90s, it was immediate jail time. So we got slick, hiding the drugs about ten feet away in a broken bottle or under a piece of trash. When a customer stopped by we would serve them from the stash. But any minute we might see blue cars hitting the corner. We studied the lights on the police cars and how the engines of Crown Victorias or Grand Marquis (police vehicles of choice) sounded in the night.

CraigyQ and I were on the block one day when we saw the jump-out boys heading our way doing about fifty-five miles an hour on a residential street. The car jumped the curb, and everyone scattered as we came out of a nearby store. CraigyQ started to run through an open field with police yelling "Freeze!" as they chased him. He purposely fell down, flinging the drugs across the grassy field. The police checked him, but he had no drugs on him so they were forced to let him go.

This episode got us thinking. We decided to move our operation to the projects on the northeast side of town. We swaggered in, took over a house by promising to pay the occupants with drugs, made a couple of threats, then stood outside on the stoop with loud music playing and our guns in plain sight stuck in our pants. Our plan worked; the other dealers in the neighborhood were furious but afraid to retaliate.

After a month or so, CraigyQ and I decided the place was too hot. We moved out without telling a soul, later learning that police raided the house just two days after we'd gone.

It wasn't too long before I started selling drugs with my girlfriend, a niece of the General. Tanea could have been a good friend, but instead I introduced her to the dope game. We would be out selling dope for days, making huge profits that put us on the top of everyone's list of people they wanted to recruit. But we didn't want to be on someone else's team or have someone else telling us how much to sell.

We would sell thousands of dollars worth of drugs weekly, but couldn't get past that level. Our plan was to buy some dope as well as get some on consignment. We spent a thousand dollars, then cut the dope and sold it in pieces for two thousand. A tidy thousand-dollar profit! We got our first consignment from a stereotypical dealer from Benton Harbor named H: huge gold chains, gold teeth, and a BMW with tinted windows. But this crack was a different color than we were used to, which made me nervous. My uncle Dave (Cameo) tried it, reporting that it was something he'd never seen before.

We decided to forget the huge profits and move back into selling at Uncle Dave Jacob's house where we could sell about a thousand dollars' worth on a good day. I also took over a two-apartment house across the street from our drug house. This was a prostitution house, as well as another place to sell drugs. I was expanding my horizons!

GOING TO DIE

One night my elementary school friend Danny came to the house with his cousin Dre. Dre hated me because he was a member of a rival gang, but they were high on crack so it didn't matter to him. We sold them probably a thousand dollars' worth of dope that night; they kept returning to pawn guns, microwaves, jewelry, and anything they could get their hands on to steal and sell. Things got ugly at about 4 a.m.

I opened the door to find a double-barreled shotgun aimed at my face. Dre—high and shaking—kept saying, "You're going to die!" This from a guy known for shooting people. He was high; he already didn't like me; and I was ranked in the gang and well-known for bringing the noise. This was a recipe for death, and I knew it.

> I opened the door to find a double-barreled shotgun aimed at my face.

They took all of our dope and the stuff they'd pawned to us, but there wasn't anything I could do with that shotgun aimed at my face and Dre shaking like a '57 Chevy. Then he saw Tanea's rings.

"Give me your rings," yelled the high, jittery guy with a shotgun aimed at me.

"You're not getting nothin' from me," she said back.

"Yeah," I thought, "you don't have a shotgun aimed at your head."

The two went back and forth for a minute or so over those rings.

"Let's go," Danny said, eager to end the standoff.

But Dre turned to me and said, too quietly, "You about to die."

"Come on, Dre," Danny hollered, distracting Dre just for a second.

I shoved Tanea into the bathroom, and we jumped in the tub, expecting a shotgun blast at any second.

But Danny and Dre ran out of the house without firing a shot, taking our drugs with them. Uncle Dave came out of the back room in shock, studying my face that reflected only my rage and fear. Without saying a word, I got up out of the tub and called a cab. I headed out to get my pistol, vowing to kill them both. I carried it loaded for days in case I saw Dre and Danny. Craig and Gotti rode around with me for a week looking for them; I vowed that I would shoot them if I ever saw them again.

Despite our illegal business dealings and brushes with death, respect was still the name of the game. Danny and Dre had disrespected me in a big way, and I needed to remedy that situation. I searched for them every day as I continued to sell drugs. It wasn't long before I got caught.

DEAD TO RIGHTS

I was selling drugs as usual at my uncle Dave's house (he's since passed away). His house was jumping day and night, but in a low-key way. Only his friends would come over and buy dope. Dave would run the dope for me and take his cut off the top, which was great protection for me.

Dave introduced me to a woman friend of his who would buy dope, then smoke it in a room we'd set aside for smokers. We figured this was a good way to keep the buyers right in the house, spending all the money they had without ever walking out the door.

Marilyn introduced Dave to a friend of hers who would come in from out of town and buy several hundred dollars' worth of dope each time she visited. I didn't trust most people, especially ones I didn't know, but my greed took over. One night while on my way to an Ice Cube concert I got word that the out-of-towner wanted to purchase a nice amount of dope from me. I got her what she wanted, asking and getting top dollar.

> I later learned my uncle Dave was offered a deal if he would give up his "source," which was me. He didn't give me up, and was sentenced to seven years in prison.

Several months later, I was busted with a pocket full of drugs. I was sentenced to jail time in the county lockup, where I sat for weeks on end. One day I was called downtown for a court appearance, which I thought might be for not paying child support. While I sat there in the cages, several people I knew from different dope sets around the city were brought in.

Then I saw my uncle Dave dragged in as well.

"They got me, Neph," he yelled to me as I sat in the cell.

The next morning we were brought into court in our county greens, and there sat the lady I had sold drugs to on that concert night months before. We had been caught in a sting operation. I was scared because people who were caught, as I was, were getting ten to fifteen years in prison.

My lawyer wanted me to take a plea bargain in return for five years in prison, but I refused. I ended up sitting in county lockup for a year before I was sentenced. I received two years with time served, and was sent to a boot camp for six months.

I later learned my uncle Dave was offered a deal if he would give up his "source," which was me. He didn't give me up and was sentenced to seven years in prison. My respect for him grew exponentially knowing he protected me at the expense of time in jail.

SHOW SOME RESPECT

Honor and respect are virtues learned and gained over time. Those in the street culture understand these core values better than most, having lived much of their lives earning, keeping, and giving respect often as a matter of life and death.

Honor is defined as "to value, respect, or highly esteem; to treat as precious, weighty, or valuable." I believe that redirecting the God-given virtues of honor and respect is possible in the street context.

I remember riding around with brothers getting drunk out of our minds on the way to do great bodily harm to a rival gang member or someone who had disrespected us. But when we rode by a church, we'd turn down the music and tell everyone to stop cussing. This was our strange attempt at respect.

Early in our urban ministry, LaDawn and I discovered the disturbing fact that many inner-city pastors didn't know how to gain the respect of the youth in their own neighborhoods. I was invited to a church several years ago with my dear friend Omar, who is now serving a life sentence in prison. We stood inside the church with the deacons, staring through the thick glass at several young men obviously selling drugs on the porch of the church. The deacons complained about their lack of respect, asking us to tell them to stop.

> We didn't tell them to stop selling drugs and quit smoking their weed. We did, however, show them respect by addressing them kindly.

Omar and I were always looking for a good fight, so we talked with the young brothers. We explained that this was a house of God and asked them to respect it. We didn't tell them to stop selling drugs and quit smoking their weed. We did, however, show them respect by addressing them kindly. We also told them that if they needed anything to come to the church. They agreed not to sell drugs outside the church anymore.

I spoke to the pastor of that church years later, and he reported that they hadn't been back selling since.

TAKE IT HOME

The shallow form of respect for God is a good place to start reaching people. And showing urban people the respect they crave is a wide open door to doing some real ministry.

1. Respect Indigenous Wisdom. Clear your mind of all that you think you know and be willing to learn from those whose street smarts and life experiences provide a unique depth of wisdom. I think this is the best approach to understanding the pulse of the community and, specifically, the needs of the person on the street.

2. Respect the Three-Foot Rule. Give people their space, understanding that often in the urban context there is a major breakdown of trust as a whole. We cannot forcefully love, moving into people's personal and emotional space without permission. Establish relationships of trust and allow the relationship to grow organically.

3. Spend Meaningful Time. Spending purposeful, meaningful time is always in order. You can never spend too much time with a person, especially in the urban context.

4. Show That You Care. No one cares how much you know unless they know how much you care, as the saying goes. Showing that you care in most cases doesn't involve money. Simple things such as attending a basketball game, helping with homework, fixing a car or bike—these are the things that count. It's easy to forget this basic truth, even in an urban setting. We are in the business of loving people, not managing programs.

5. Commit to Real Talk. There is no quicker way to overcome racial and economic barriers than by being transparent and straightforward in conversation. As God leads, unpack your story with focus on his redemptive power. This will open opportunities to show people that you bleed too.

CROSSFIRE

Often it's when the world comes crashing down that God clears a path.

The correctional system did nothing to correct me. I was adept at using the system for my own ends, getting what I wanted no matter what it took.

As I sat in jail after my arrest for drug possession, a member of some kind of drug task force visited me. The guy said that if I gave them names and worked with them to reveal other drug dealers, they would shorten the time I spent in jail. I agreed, thinking only about getting my freedom back. Besides, I never liked those guys from Detroit anyway.

Mark, the undercover cop, and his boss picked me up in a black, old-school Camero and drove me to a part of Grand Rapids I didn't know. They talked about the rules for snitches, and I talked about the rules for buying drugs: be picky about what you buy or the dealers will figure you out right away. We even set up a buy; Mark rode along as I bought drugs from the Detroit dealers.

My show of good faith brought about my release from jail. I agreed to live at my mother's house in exchange for continuing to supply them with info about the dealers in the area. Fat chance! As soon as they dropped me off I left to hook up with my gang brothers and resume my leadership role.

I vowed not to keep an upcoming court date, but my family and friends recommended I do so because missing it meant escalating trouble with the judicial system. I understood escalating trouble, so I showed up in court only to be arrested for not holding up my end of the snitch bargain. In the end, I took a plea bargain on the drug possession charge. This included spending an additional six months in jail with time served and six months in a halfway house. Not a bad deal considering I could have spent a decade in jail.

THE HALFWAY LIFE

I got along fine at the halfway house. Alternative Directions was located smack in the middle of the war zone between my gang and our rival. It was just a few minutes' walk from my grandfather's church and my home. We were supposed to be out during the day looking for jobs, filling out applications, or signing up for school. Right. I was out running my gang and connecting with my old buddies.

> The people in charge liked me. . . . I had their respect, and quickly gained respect from those I didn't know.

We also took classes on anger management, worked toward a GED, and attended sessions where crime victims visited to help put a human face on the crimes we had committed. I even facilitated a couple of these sessions later in life.

My leadership capabilities came into play at the halfway house. The people in charge liked me, and I knew a lot of the cats on my floor from the neighborhood. I had their respect and quickly gained respect from those I didn't know. If there was some trouble, the guys in charge got me.

They'd say, "I don't want this guy getting kicked out. Would you mind talking to him?" I'd jump right into the beef and straighten things out. I got cool with a couple of the guys in charge who must have seen something good in me.

But their respect wasn't enough. I zeroed in on the one guy who wasn't so solid and used him for my own ends. I told him that we could come to an agreement: my supplying him with women and his letting me have a little freedom. Our nights got to be a routine: I'd set him up with a female and leave him alone, then I'd do my own thing. This usually meant handling some business with my girlfriend and structuring some drug situations and gang-related business.

I was a master manipulator, coming back drunk to a place that would throw me back in jail in a heartbeat for using even a drop of alcohol. I went so far as to have a pistol hidden at the halfway house.

My time there, however, wasn't a completely degenerate mess. I ended up with a job as an assistant to a janitor at Jordan College. Kevin and I got along fine. He and others treated me like a regular guy instead of the ex-con they all knew I was.

While sweeping the hallways and cleaning bathrooms, I met MaLinda Sapp, wife of gospel singer and pastor Rev. Marvin Sapp. MaLinda was on staff at Jordan College and treated me like she treated everyone else—with respect and kindness. She had an openness to finding opportunities to share in my life and show kindness to me. Despite her kindness, I was still full of garbage and darkness and determined to go my own way.

> MaLinda . . . treated me like she treated everyone else—with respect and kindness. She had an openness to finding opportunities to share in my life and show kindness to me.

MaLinda Sapp passed away recently from cancer, leaving behind her husband and three children. Her loss devastated me as I remembered her kindness in those dark days. She made sure she gave everyone a chance.

FRANCIS STREET SIEGE

Despite the kindnesses of people like MaLinda at Jordan College and the good guys in charge of the halfway house, the gang was still my life. I knew nothing else, craving the power, money, and respect that came with gang leadership. As soon as I got out of the halfway house, I was back on Francis Street selling drugs, using violence, drinking, using women, and running my part of the gang. But now I had a new plan. I decided to form the Francis Street Mob, a subsidiary of the national gang that I loved so much.

The Francis Street Mob had its beginnings while I was in jail. I had been grooming my brother Mark (nicknamed Shark), and several others as my officers. While still in the halfway house, I bought large amounts of drugs and supplied dealers on Francis Street, solidifying my leadership and power base. The minute I got out, I was back to stay. Our crime became more organized, with gang members selling drugs, running a prostitution house, and recruiting new members.

We officially were organized as the Francis Street Mob, a small portion of which still exists today. While my brother wasn't interested in joining, he was around to participate in retribution events. We had a small army of about fifty people ready to put an end to the rival gangs. But Francis Street was in a state of siege. We were one part of a national gang surrounded on all sides by members of rival gangs who had vowed to kill us if given the chance. And I was the leader.

> Francis Street was in a state of siege. We were one part of a national gang surrounded on all sides by members of rival gangs who had vowed to kill us if given the chance. And I was the leader.

I was still reporting to Alternative Directions, but I couldn't even walk down the street to get there. The rival gang kept watch for me and would kill me immediately on sight. I couldn't get to the halfway house, couldn't walk to the corner store I'd been visiting since I was a child. I depended on my officers to take care of business, while I mostly laid low and took care of educating and training new recruits.

My cousin Rick (Ricardo 2X) walked up the hill to the store one day, only to come flying back with our rivals right behind him. No one was around to help as Rick banged on doors and tried to get through windows. He eventually found an open window, but as he climbed through, one of our rivals attacked him with a machete, severely wounding his arm. Events like this only served to strengthen our resolve.

> Shots flew whenever we showed our noses. We were in a state of siege.

My officers were Mike Stone, a former Marine sniper; my friend Boony; my god-brother Kenny; and my cousin Vern the Concern. We'd send Mike up to the rooftops sometimes to take aim at our rivals. His skills came in especially handy during a day that put the Francis Street Mob into the spotlight for our fifteen minutes of fame.

The news media called it the "Old West Shoot-Out on Francis Street" because of all the crossfire between gangs that went on that day. We'd shoot from the houses at them; they'd shoot at us from their cars as they drove by. Bullets were flying everywhere, bringing in the cops and news media. We developed a plan that called for us to drop to the floor GI Joe-style when the shooting started; we'd lie on the floor and shoot out the door at our rivals. When I look back now, it's hard to believe any of us survived that day and the weeks of violence before and after.

Everyone was wild and violent in those days, living a fast-paced life without any thought to the reality and consequences of their actions. After awhile, we became sitting ducks. Our rivals became more organized, thanks to better leadership and more members, and they determined to shut us down. Surrounding blocks were controlled by them, so shots flew whenever we showed our noses. We were in a state of siege.

Even the drug addicts wouldn't come to Francis Street. We had no way to make money, thanks to our shrinking drug trade, and we couldn't even move. Guys wanted to go home; even my mother left with my younger sister and brother.

These dangerous times came to a head the day my brother Mark got shot. Our gang had a code word we used to tell everyone it was time to scatter and regroup at a specified location. We used the word during a raid by the rival gang; we scattered and began to rendezvous, but someone was missing. Mark the Shark wasn't with us. Those shots we heard as we ran must have been for him.

Instead of scattering with us, Mark had stayed behind to protect his girl-friend and their baby daughter. Our rivals found him and let loose a barrage of shots. He took one in the chest.

I was devastated, furious, ready to cast blame. But Mike Stone cast it back on me. He blamed me for Ricardo 2X's injury, Kenny and Titus being shot earlier, and now for Mark. I was so angry I could only cry. But I wasn't going to take the blame. I blamed the gang. The gang hadn't sent reinforce-ments, resupplied us with guns, helped reestablish our drug trade, or given us money.

In that moment of grief, anger, and disbelief, I disowned the gang. I left the group that had given me identity and love and a reason to die. I vowed to leave the group that I believed had given me my life.

TAKE IT HOME

How can churches, especially those in urban settings, help bring ex-cons back into the fold of faith and build a useful life? The needs extend to their families as well. And when the moment of crisis comes—when the betrayal happens or when the gang drops the ball—will the church be there to help? Here are several suggestions.

1. Establish a Mentoring Program. Mentors can help kids stay out of gangs and away from crime, help adults repatriate into the community after prison, and help women avoid debilitating relationships. Mentoring programs offer a wide array of options that churches can tailor to best meet the needs of their communities.

2. Offer Life Skills Training. Churches can offer workshops on anger management, financial management, housekeeping skills, reading and math skills, and even counseling services.

3. Provide Parenting Resources. We all can use help with parenting, but those jumping back into parenting may need extra advice. Churches can offer parenting how-to classes, programs such as Head Start and MOPS, before/after school care, and support groups of all kinds.

4. Offer Educational Opportunities. Many ex-cons need a high school diploma, so GED classes are helpful. Job training and vocational skills are useful as are school supplies offered free or at reduced cost.

5. Provide Basic Health Care Services. Blood pressure and blood sugar monitoring, foot care, dental care, and prenatal care are all options.

6. Become a Safe Haven. The church can become the safe haven for any community. Open doors mean folks are coming inside and finding help and peace. Your church may consider a food pantry, clothing closet, hang-out place for youth, and provide a free meal.

PART 3

THE JOURNEY

12

THE GREAT ESCAPE

The powerful draw of freedom can lead to the pursuit of life.

My brother Mark survived the gunshot to his chest. He had spent years lifting weights and working out, so when the small-caliber bullet struck, it didn't do as much damage as it could have. Mark still has the bullet lodged in his chest today. The doctors say that his muscle saved his life. I say that God spared his life for a greater cause.

He recovered, but I couldn't recover from the damage done that day. I had dropped my flag (denounced the gang), which meant huge repercussions to come. The gang had been my surrogate family; everything I did and learned had come through them. The money I made, the power I had, the respect I gained were all tied to the gang. Yet now my emotions were mixed as I mentally and emotionally pulled away. Strangely, I felt the same emotions leaving the gang that I had felt leaving my mama's house a few years earlier: fear, pride, and helplessness.

But this leaving had much more serious consequences. The Francis Street Mob was leaderless and rudderless. Some guys stayed with the Mob while others swore their allegiance to the larger gang that was over us. Others were angry at gang life and the violence and walked away.

Of course word got back to the General about what had gone down. I knew my actions required him to make a move, which he did. According to one of my guys, during a Friday afternoon meeting the General said the code word for "hit" and said my nickname, which was Bat. This meant everyone present was issued a mandate to kill me on sight.

MARKED FOR THE HIT

Every gang has a set of rules by which they operate, whether verbal or in some kind of notebook that lists all the gang's laws, codes, prayers, rituals, symbols, and whatever else they find important. My gang's book of "standard operating procedures" included the 101 key codes used to disguise the major actions of the gang. There were codes for everything from the code of silence, till death do us part, various kinds of retributions, and hits. When the General said the code word, everyone knew that a hit on me had been issued.

> The General's orders had to be obeyed with no questions asked. Gang members swear a blood oath to obey all rules; and if they don't, the punishment can be death.

They also knew that the General's orders had to be obeyed with no questions asked. Gang members swear a blood oath to obey all rules; and if they don't, the punishment can be death. This is true in all major gangs to this day.

The word on the street was that all my former gang buddies were looking for me. Being more arrogant than most and so hurt by the recent events, I pretty much ignored the warning. Instead of holing up in fear, I visited the clubs, walked the streets, and almost dared someone to come at me. I carried a pistol with me, always ready for anything. In fact, I sort of liked the bragging rights that came with having a hit placed on me.

I ran into several lower-level guys during that time, but none of them tried anything with me. I even saw Gotti, groomed to take over the General's spot, but he didn't do anything either, perhaps out of his own mixed feelings over the events on Francis Street. Even today, I believe we have a bond that cannot be broken. He was the only person from the gang who reached out to me when my brother got shot.

But then the guys started going door to door looking for me. The final straw came when they knocked on my mom's door to ask where I was. She came crying to me, begging me to leave. My aunts were with her, crying and carrying on about how I was going to die. I was cold; I brushed them off, telling them I'd handle it.

They got reinforcements in the form of my grandfather. When he sent word to say I'd better leave Grand Rapids, I took note. My family was serious about wanting me to live. I guess I got serious about living then, too, because it wasn't long before a carload of us headed south to Georgia and a brand-new life.

NEW WORLD

My mom and two of her sisters sat in the front seat, while Kenny, Vern, and I sat in the back of that crowded, midsize car. Talk about a long trip! We were headed to my uncle Vern's house — father to my cousin Vern and former husband of my aunt — on McAfee Road in Decatur, Georgia.

We arrived amid the wet heat of the South with little money and no plans. Uncle Vern met us out front of his house, hugging us all and making us feel welcome. He had gathered a bunch of girls to come over that night to welcome us, so we enjoyed that first night quite a bit. We ate good Southern cooking and basked in our new freedom.

"We're going to own this town," we crowed, thinking of the gun we'd smuggled into our meager luggage. We kept quiet, though, knowing my mom and the aunts would pitch a fit if they found out. They left the next morning to return home.

After we spent a hot and muggy Georgia night sleeping on mattresses in the one bedroom, Uncle Vern rousted us out of bed. We shuffled outside, barely awake and already hot, to stare at a bunch of trees growing in the backyard. Our job was to cut down those trees, and there was no getting around it. Uncle Vern had plans for us that did not include lying around the house all day and staying up all night. We either had to get a job and pay him room and board or work in the yard to earn our keep. We got to work.

> I felt protected and honored that someone would take up for me that way. I will always love Uncle Vern for what he did for me.

It was no secret that Uncle Vern loved his weed. We often awoke to the smell of marijuana wafting through the house. He worked third shift, and we occasionally heard him coming home. We'd hear him— at first faintly and then louder as he walked up the driveway—chanting, "Can't wait, can't wait, can't wait." Come to find out, Uncle Vern's excitement had nothing to do with us. He just couldn't wait to get to that weed he had hidden under his bed.

Uncle Vern was big on family. He took us in and welcomed us, becoming a father figure to Kenny and me, and building a relationship with his son Vern. One incident endeared Uncle Vern to me even more. Just a few days after we arrived, I learned that Mark Morgan, my biological father, lived less than twenty minutes from Uncle Vern's house. I called him and asked if I could visit him. He said he'd visit me that night, but he never showed. I waited for hours to see my birth father who couldn't be bothered. I was hurt and angry, so maybe it was best he never visited the entire time I was in Georgia.

Uncle Vern, a childhood friend of Mark's, called and let him have it with every name in the book. I felt protected and honored that someone would take up for me that way. I will always love Uncle Vern for what he did for me.

Our time there wasn't always a smooth ride, though, and Uncle Vern would step in to diffuse the situation. Vern loved to tease, and he began teasing Kenny. Kenny was missing home (he was only about seventeen at the time) and his girlfriend, who would soon have his baby. Vern started joking about Kenny's girlfriend stepping out on him, until one day Kenny had had enough. He pulled that gun we'd brought down, aiming it right at Vern. I couldn't get Kenny to stand down; he was ready to shoot Vern right on the spot. Uncle Vern walked in and began talking low and easy to Kenny, slowly walking toward him. He kept talking until he moved in swiftly and took Kenny down to the ground with gun in hand.

> Gangbanging started to recede to the back of my mind as hope replaced the violence and darkness that had characterized my life for so long.

The upside to life in the South was the cooking. Uncle Vern's girlfriend could cook up a storm: fried chicken scalded in grease to perfection, rice, grits, fried potatoes. We'd get up to a breakfast of leftovers from the day before, looking forward to more of the same that day. The food was just goodness!

Another revelation occurred when I took the MARTA (public transit) into downtown Atlanta. I loved wandering around the city; I guess I was fascinated by this new place so far from my blighted urban neighborhood. I was stunned to see black folks who owned businesses and even buildings. I knew there were folks like that in Grand Rapids, but we had no exposure to people of color doing things at that level.

I saw no racial divide, either; no open, blatant racism in Atlanta. I saw black and white folks doing things together. I'm not sure what I expected in this Southern metropolis—perhaps even worse racism than I saw at home in the North—but what I saw opened my mind to a world of possibilities for my life. Gangbanging started to recede to the back of my mind as hope replaced the violence and darkness that had characterized my life for so long.

I thought that maybe I could do something other than pushing dope and banging. I dreamed of doing promotional work for rappers, setting up and advertising concerts and the like.

I dreamed!

COST OF FREEDOM

Leaving the gang life is extremely dangerous, but it is doable. I left, and I have friends across the country who have walked away from their gangs without repercussions. The key is understanding gang life and its values.

I know of a pastor in Guatemala whose ministry was to reach out to gang members. The violence in his target neighborhood got so bad that the pastor contacted a top-ranking international gang leader for a meeting. The leader accepted his offer and had the pastor blindfolded and brought to a cave. When the blindfold was removed, the pastor found himself surrounded by men carrying machine guns.

> If a banger wants to commit to religion, I will let him leave. But if he shows inconsistencies, I will have no mercy on him.

"What can I do for you, preacher?" the leader asked.

The pastor started unpacking a plan to clean up their city, asking for the gang leader's help. The pastor asked for permission to offer young men the opportunity for a new life outside the gang for those who want to follow Christ.

The gang leader paused, then made this profound statement: "If a banger wants to commit to religion, I will let him leave. But if he shows inconsistencies, I will have no mercy on him."

A good friend of mine, José Valez, is a former leader of the Spanish Cobras gang in Chicago. He joined the gang at age thirteen, rising quickly through the ranks to become the leader. He watched more than a hundred of his friends and family members die and had many run-ins with the law himself. After being shot in front of his home, José walked away from gang life.

Today, José speaks to students and mentors young people about staying away from gangs. He provides advice to parents who suspect their children are succumbing to gang lifestyles. My point is this: If José can walk away from being a banger, anyone can.

Even the roughest guys have values. Most bangers understand and respect the concept of commitment, which is where the church and those working in the hood can start.

TAKE IT HOME

What follows is a basic list for working with gangs in your community.

Connect with Local Gangs

1. Show respect for the gangs by showing basic love and kindness.
2. Be willing to talk with and listen to gang leaders when the time comes. Building relationships based on trust is key.
3. Work with (or create) community job programs to get bangers off the street.
4. Because many gang members are also selling drugs, they have some attributes of any business owner. Find opportunities to hear their dreams and desires; don't overlook their skills.
5. Offer gang members another life through Christ, and another way to live through mentoring and modeling.
6. Open the doors to your church or youth center to give kids a place to hang out, feel safe, and eat a hot meal.
7. Don't try to relate to gang members. Just listen and build relationships.

8. Whatever you commit to, do it!

9. When the opportunity comes to share the gospel, go for it!

Help Kids Avoid Gangs

1. Show genuine acceptance to your children, which will help prevent them from searching for it in a gang.

2. Offer other activities such as sports, music lessons, church events, and opportunities for exploration.

3. Monitor after-school activities by being present or with adequate daycare to prevent opportunities for kids to get into trouble.

4. Create an environment that encourages and celebrates a healthy respect for education and a work ethic.

5. Monitor *all* social network conversations, pictures, and videos. When we (gang specialists) look to see what the latest trends in gang activities are, we comb through social media sites.

6. Know who your kids are hanging out with; invite them over and get to know them.

7. Teach media awareness and filter what youth are exposed to. Youth and adults alike are becoming desensitized to sexual perversion and violence. They are learning enough to be dangerous, thanks to movies, video games, and YouTube.

8. Model the life of authentic Christianity, which is much more than a bunch of rules to follow. Rather, it's a lifestyle of surrendering to the God of the universe.

9. Be willing to relocate if necessary to keep kids away from gang recruiters.

10. The reality is that if kids are wearing gang colors, parents are the ones buying the clothing. Forgive, but don't enable.

11. Set firm rules about drinking, drugs, curfew, schoolwork, and so forth.

12. No one writes the same symbols or numbers over and over unless they value those symbols and numbers. If you see symbols or numbers repeatedly in your kids' stuff, immediately check with local law enforcement to determine if those things are gang related.

13

THAT NEXT HORIZON

We'll search strange places in our quest for identity.

My world was expanding, and my dreams were coming true. I enjoyed downtown Atlanta, with its mix of races, energy, and freedom. I had my eyes and nose wide open to what was going on. My favorite spot was Five Points, a district of Atlanta considered to be the center of the city.

Five Points started as the intersection of two Creek Indian trails, later becoming home to Atlanta's first grocery store and post office. Before the advent of urban sprawl, Five Points was the hub of downtown Atlanta, home to Rich's Department Store, cultural venues, and many small businesses.

My destination was often the Five Points MARTA station, the largest in the area. Students, shoppers, and businesspeople made the station busy and energetic. I got a job picking up trash at the nearby Georgia Dome, home field of the Atlanta Falcons football team and venue for many events.

I made five dollars an hour, which helped me begin taking care of myself. I was able to pay Uncle Vern for letting me stay at his house, plus I had a little spending money. The most amazing thing about this time is that I was making money by completely legal means. I got a paycheck, paid taxes, and didn't have to worry about being busted on the job.

Atlanta was a melting pot for all kinds of people and religions. It was crazy how many people were touting their beliefs in that city. I had gone to just one church in my life pastored by my grandfather, so my exposure was somewhat limited. But here in this southern metropolis, I came into contact with the Nubian Nation, Sunni Islam, Hebrew Israelites, and plenty of Southern Baptists.

Hebrew Israelites believe themselves descendants of the ancient Israelites, though most don't consider themselves Jewish. Made up mostly of African-Americans, the group incorporates Jewish practices to varying levels according to which subgroup they belong. I became interested in the group because they seemed to be the most knowledgeable about matters of faith and culture. They shared my frustration with white people and some of the racism I had experienced. Yet I never joined because I could not get beyond the idea that their leader/preacher needed to use curse words to get his point across.

STEPPING UP TO THE BOTTOM RUNG

I still loved rap music, dancing, mixing, and deejaying. As I sought out that world, I met a rapper named MCR (real name Ralph), who was trying to record a tape at his Five Points studio. We hit it off immediately as I told him about the record deal I'd had in Grand Rapids with the group I was in, Mack 10. Our record, titled "The Whole Ten Yards," was hardcore gangsta rap that advocated violence against rivals, women, and the world. We got into altercations fairly often over the content and I never made a dime off that recording, but at least it gave me bragging rights.

MCR was just as heavy into rap and also into the production end of things. He said he'd teach me how to run a studio, which I latched onto immediately. We had a small studio that created pretty good sound using old-school eight-track and reel-to-reel tapes, good enough for demo tapes at least. Groups and individuals would come in to make their tape, then try to peddle it to the big producers.

We would get visits from the emerging group OutKast, a duo based in East Point, Georgia. I remember meeting Andre "Andre 3000" Benjamin and Antwan "Big Boi" Patton when they came down to chill with the "little guys." They would stand outside the studio booth and give guys daps (handshakes), encouraging them to keep it going. We would hang with Jermaine Dupri, a hip-hop artist with the record label So-So Def (his label has had multiple platinum albums), and I remember artists such as Usher, Monica, and Illegal (now disbanded) all looking to get in the industry at the same time. In the early 1990s, Atlanta was what Motown was in the '60s and '70s, and we were in the middle of it all! (OutKast is now one of the most successful hip-hop groups with six Grammy Awards and over twenty-five million records sold; Usher recently took home two American Music Awards, while his protégé, Justin Bieber, took home four.)

MCR and I recorded our own tape, a remarkably racist and antiwhite tape that was horrible for its message. We created it over a week, bringing in guest artists to record with us.

Rather than studying marketing how-to manuals or attending seminars, we devised our own plan to sell our music. We walked to the nearest street corner and began hawking copies of our one little tape (these were the days before CDs). I found myself on the street corners once again, but this time several things were in my favor. First of all, the weather was better. Very few blizzards in Atlanta. Second, I didn't have to run every time I saw a police officer. I didn't have to memorize the sounds of police cars, didn't have to duck the undercover cops. My wares wouldn't land me in jail.

MCR and I made enough money to pay our bills (sometimes). I moved out of Uncle Vern's house out in Decatur and into MCR's office space in downtown Atlanta. We were on the way to bigger things, but in the meantime lived in a small office space, slept on cots, and used a communal bathroom in the building. This was our home for about three months.

NEVER LOOKING BACK

The two of us were going places; we had big dreams and the drive to accomplish them. We were slowly gaining clients who used our production and marketing services, and slowly making a name for ourselves. We opened another demo business in Decatur and hired two young guys to hang out at the studio to run it, though we chose to stay downtown, eventually renting a house in the Five Points area. We often couldn't afford electricity, but MCR Productions—and me and MCR himself—had a home.

> The two of us were going places; we had big dreams and the drive to accomplish them.

Once again we strategized our own marketing plan. We moved from the street corners to the area strip joints, where we hung out in an effort to get our name out there. We worked to create a buzz, getting the DJs to announce that MCR Productions was "in the house" when we walked in the door. We got them to play our tapes, introducing the strip club crowd to our signature sound, as well as our clients' sounds.

This was a culture I knew well. I was in familiar territory on the streets of Atlanta and in the clubs that dotted the area. While I wasn't dealing drugs, I was dealing a product—hip-hop music and the dream of stardom—that people wanted. We sold thousands of our own tapes and created hundreds of demo packages for up-and-coming artists.

MCR and I felt on the verge of something big. We sat in the strip clubs and dance clubs and dreamed of our big break. We had watched OutKast and some of the other groups take off, and felt that we could ride that wave. I had a real hunger for more that got hold of me right in the middle of my gut. It was that hunger for money and to do something really big that took me down a new path.

Atlanta is a great place to hang out on porches in the warm evenings. So many houses don't have air conditioning, so the cool evenings are spent outside. My girlfriend, MCR, a few others, and I lounged on the porch one night as we watched a large, fancy car pull up to the sidewalk.

A well-dressed dude got out and started a conversation. We got through the introductions—his name was Rudy—before he started about how he had a grind, a hustle, that he needed help with. I was interested, especially when he promised to finance the promotion company I had in mind to start. I got in Rudy's fancy car, and we drove to a place to talk. And that man could talk.

He needed a bodyguard to help him get in and out of places, to help him do what he needed to do—as he said, "to keep it moving." I fell into the trap of promised wealth and power once again, vowing to do whatever Rudy needed in exchange for future financing of my dream.

I never really went back to that house in Five Points. I had left my girlfriend standing on the porch when I got in Rudy's car—a girl who had dropped out of college to hang with me—and I never went back. It's hard to believe I left her, literally, standing on the porch, but I did. And I left MCR stranded in our business as well. I returned and packed a few things, said goodbye to my friends and her, got in the car with Rudy, and never looked back. I have never seen that girl again, and I never saw MCR again either, despite trying to locate him.

It was that hunger for money and to do something really big that took me down a new path.

Rudy and I hit the road. He traveled often to places such as Washington DC, and Richmond, Virginia, cities I had never seen. I truly didn't know what Rudy was into—obviously I didn't want to know—but I watched his back all the way. He was an old-school hustler making mysterious deliveries and doing "concert promotion," whatever that was. I was along for the ride, wherever it took me. Surprisingly, it took me just a bit closer to huge changes in my life.

WHO ARE THEY?

I moved from the streets of the second largest city in Michigan to the streets of the largest city in Georgia, but I still asked the same question: Who am I? My new life didn't answer the fundamental questions in my life. The new religions I saw didn't either.

> The church must be in the business of providing identity to the broken.

I had bought into the lie of the streets— that I was nothing but a banger, that the streets are all there is, that I could never leave the streets—so thoroughly that I got lost in it. My brief glimpses of hope in Georgia were quickly replaced with stepping back into a life of strip clubs and violence.

Now that I'm on the other side, I realize that the church must be in the business of providing identity to the broken. The church as a whole, as well as individuals within the church, must be convinced that the power of the Holy Spirit can transform anyone into who God wants them to be. The church is responsible for reeducating the lost.

Imagine that everything around you is pushing you to believe that you are nothing but a killer and a thug. Imagine that all you see and read directs you to believe the lie that women are sex objects, that wealth brings happiness, or that power and respect are the most important things in life. How could you possibly believe otherwise?

I believe that God designed each of us with greatness in mind. Therefore, the church and its members (yes, you and me) must invest in the lives of those immersed in street life. I use the word *invest* intentionally, because I believe that if the seed of God's love is invested in even one life, the harvest will be plentiful and last for generations. Investment in lives is what revamps our urban centers and revolutionizes our communities.

We humans were not created for sin. God created us in his image and likeness, and he is not sinful. However, sin came into the world, thanks to the choices of one man and woman (Gen. 3:1–7). Despite our current sinful condition, God's intent for our lives doesn't change. He still desires our love, obedience, and full commitment.

TAKE IT HOME

Pastor Paul Hontz of Central Wesleyan Church in Holland, Michigan, uses a two-word model that we at The EDGE have recently adopted: *invest* and *invite*. The idea is that we spend time investing in individuals, then we invite them to go on a journey of restoration and engage in a lasting relationship with the true and living King.

The Investment

Psalm 139:13–14: "For you created my inmost being; you knit me together in my mother's womb. I praise you because I am fearfully and wonderfully made; your works are wonderful, I know that full well."

Ephesians 2:10: "We are God's workmanship, created in Christ Jesus to do good works, which God prepared in advance for us to do."

Investment Summary

1. We are God's handiwork, through Christ.
2. We are made with greatness in mind.
3. Each of us is uniquely crafted by God.
4. God doesn't make junk.
5. God created each of us with a purpose in mind.

The Invitation

Psalm 82:2–4: "How long will you defend the unjust and show partiality to the wicked? Defend the cause of the weak and fatherless; maintain the rights of the poor and oppressed. Rescue the weak and needy; deliver them from the hand of the wicked."

Psalm 9:8–10: "He will judge the world in righteousness; he will govern the peoples with justice. The LORD is a refuge for the oppressed, a stronghold in times of trouble. Those who know your name trust in you, for you, LORD, have never forsaken those who seek you."

Luke 10:26–28: "'What is written in the Law?' he replied. 'How do you read it?' He answered, 'Love the Lord your God with all your heart and with all your soul and with all your strength and with all your mind'; and, 'Love your neighbor as yourself.' 'You have answered correctly,' Jesus replied. 'Do this and you will live.'"

Invitation Summary

1. God calls us to help, defend, and uphold the oppressed and needy.
2. God is a refuge for those in need, including bangers who cry out to him.
3. God promises to deliver those who seek his name.
4. Helping the needy and oppressed is a command.
5. Loving your neighbor (bangers, addicts, homeless) brings life.

14

TOTAL LOSS

God often prepares a heart by removing all it cares for.

God tugged at my heart with a pistol and a vest.

I had been traveling with Rudy for several months around the South as he did business in the bigger cities. I played my role as bodyguard to the hilt. I checked out places we visited for possible enemies. I escorted Rudy into his meetings. I stood around looking tough, and occasionally I had to actually be tough.

There were times I had to push people away from Rudy to protect him from possible attack. I checked Rudy's guests for weapons, made threats when needed, and pulled out my pistol if warranted.

We made a good pair: Rudy the Hustler and Bat the Bodyguard.

SHOWDOWN

One day we were invited to a home in Durham, North Carolina, to do some business. It was an informal meeting with some guys, but my posture was still "I'm here for a purpose." This was a chill time with some of Rudy's friends. We were listening to instrumentals while Rudy was in another room doing whatever he did. The man in charge had several dudes around him, one who obviously didn't like the look of me. We stared each other down for a couple of minutes, daring one another to make a move. I wasn't about to move because that day—for a reason only God knew—I wasn't strapped. Normally my pistol went everywhere with me, but not this day.

Rudy was talking a mile a minute, which was strange for him. I listened to him babbling for a while, wondering what the deal was, until I heard him say, "You know what he's here for? You know what he's here to do?"

Rudy was gesturing toward me, perhaps hinting that I would be taking care of business right away. I looked at the guy across from me. I don't think I'd ever seen anyone with such a cold demeanor. He was shaking with fury, his cold eyes darting back and forth. I wasn't sure what was going down when he got up from the table and hustled upstairs. I mentally sighed in relief, thinking he'd left for good. But he quickly returned with a pistol and a bullet-proof vest. He tossed them to me, then stood glaring at me. This was a look of challenge. He was challenging me to a modern version of an Old West shoot-out.

"What you goin' do?" he grunted. He was in my face, his eyes moving crazy and his awful breath just about making me sick. All eyes in the room turned to me.

Any other time I would have relished a shoot-out, especially with a dude so obviously arrogant as this one. Everybody stared at me, at the vest and pistol, and back at the other bodyguard.

I wavered in indecision as I shrugged on the vest. This could be the end of my life, I thought. I knew this hard-eyed, seasoned fighter would take my life if he had even half a chance. But in that moment I intuitively knew that I didn't want this action.

For the first time in my gang-banging career I said to myself, "This vest and pistol isn't for me." I took off the vest and sat down again in that North Carolina hustler's living room. I'd faced off with cats many times, so I don't think it was fear that caused me to back down. But I looked at this guy, took off my vest, and set down the pistol.

The dude laughed at me. I didn't take people laughing at me very well, but that day I did. Rudy stared at me like I'd grown two heads. I stared back, wondering what I had just done. I felt like the shepherd boy David putting on King Saul's armor before going out to fight the giant Goliath. It just didn't fit. Just as David took off that armor, I had taken off the bullet-proof vest that might have protected me from the bullets of the enemy. I didn't want to fight anymore. I felt like this identity just wasn't me.

This from the guy who was convinced everybody should be a gang member; I was convinced my mother should be a gang member. I was convinced everybody should be a banger, everybody should be all into the violent thing.

> I didn't want to fight anymore. I felt like this identity just wasn't me.

Soon after, Rudy and I left the house. That event turned my heart just enough to see a new way for my life. Rudy and I never spoke of that day again.

FROM THE LOWEST POINT

Not long after that incident, I began to slide. Rudy and I remained in North Carolina as he continued to work his hustle, promote concerts, and make his mysterious deliveries. We made those deliveries in a stripped-down U-Haul-like vehicle, which became my home most of the time.

We were used to having a good time. There were girls all the time, lots of money, and parties and events we attended. One by one, however, all my enjoyment of those things went away. I just wasn't into the life anymore.

I stopped eating as well, declaring myself a vegetarian. This from the guy who loved his barbeque ribs, fried chicken, and fried catfish! Sometimes I'd go two or three days with very little food. As I think about it now, my loss of enjoyment and refusing to eat were probably due to depression. Perhaps I was mourning what I sensed was the loss of my former life that had brought me so much respect and joy. Perhaps I knew that my days as a banger and hustler were coming to an end.

> Now I know that God can take away the vices in anyone's life to make room for the new life he has planned. But then it seemed like everything I'd done and worked for was disappearing, and I didn't understand why.

All I knew was that I didn't belong there anymore. I was no longer the ruthless individual who could pull a gun in a heartbeat, beat down a rival, or enact retribution for a real or imagined slight.

God clearly was working in my life, though I didn't have a clue. Now I know that God can take away the vices in anyone's life to make room for the new life he has planned. But then it seemed like everything I'd done and worked for was disappearing, and I didn't understand why.

My life hit its lowest point early one morning. I woke up in my usual bed—an appliance box in the back of our delivery truck; Rudy was sleeping in the warm bed of a girl he'd spent the night with.

I had a few pillows and blankets in that box, along with a couple pairs of pants and shirts that fit into one small burgundy duffle bag. The shadow was lifted from my eyes in that dawn light. I was homeless, penniless, and fearful of what my boss was capable of. I think I regretted the decisions that brought me there, including leaving MCR and my girlfriend on the porch in Atlanta. I knew for sure that I was done with Rudy and the South.

I packed my bag with everything I owned and took off in the early morning light. I snuck away from my life of violence and crime. I asked the first person I saw how to get to the nearest bus station, and began walking that way. I used the few coins in my pocket to make a collect call home.

"Mama, I need to come home," I said to her as I stood in a dirty, North Carolina bus station. "It's time for me to come home, and I need help."

She—and God—heard my plea. She and my aunts and uncles scraped together the money to pay for a bus ticket. I arrived home several days later, a confused, broken, and empty young man. I was just twenty-two years old.

BRINGING HEALING

The street life takes its toll on a dweller's mental and emotional state. It's akin to those who have served in the military and engaged in active combat, experiencing one horrific thing after another. Many experience post-traumatic stress disorder which the National Institute of Mental Health defines as "an anxiety disorder that some people get after seeing or living through a dangerous event."

These events can be anything: childhood physical and/or sexual abuse, rape, a terrible car accident, being attacked or shot at, military duty, living in constant fear, a natural disaster, and so on. Danger brings fear, and fear triggers a fight-or-flight response that is designed to protect a person from harm. In PTSD, the reaction is warped, causing people to feel stressed or scared (and releasing those "danger" chemicals) even when there is no danger.

Those of us who have lived and breathed the street life can experience PTSD because of the constant violence and danger we faced. Gang life is a natural road to PTSD, thanks to the need for hyper vigilance, random acts of violence, and the constant fight-or-flight response chemicals coursing through the body.

> Gang life is a natural road to PTSD, thanks to the need for hyper vigilance, random acts of violence, and the constant fight-or-flight response chemicals coursing through the body.

Symptoms can include flashbacks; dreams about the event(s); avoiding activities once enjoyed; trouble concentrating; difficulty maintaining close relationships; irritability or anger; or self-destructive behaviors, including thoughts of suicide, hopelessness, and overwhelming guilt or shame.

I have experienced a number of PTSD symptoms: flashbacks; nightmares; difficulty concentrating; substance abuse; feeling alienated and alone; loss of interest in activities and life in general; irritability; outbursts of anger; jumpiness; being easily startled; and avoiding activities, places, thoughts, or feelings that reminded me of a trauma.

> Welcoming urban sufferers of PTSD—young and old, male and female—can become one way to reach out in the community.

Thunderstorms were the worst, but any loud noise that resembled a gunshot would leave my heart racing. Years later I would suffer great fear of going into hostile areas to do street ministry; I didn't know how I would respond to a dude acting tough or being disrespectful. For years I rehearsed in my mind what I would do to avoid hurting someone if I were to get into an altercation. This may seem extreme, but when a person lives for years responding on impulse, retraining is a must. I still concentrate my thoughts on those things that are pure, righteous, and peaceful.

The urban setting presents a number of barriers to receiving treatment for PTSD. There may be limited access to mental health services, difficulty in finding transportation to and paying for counseling services, and general lack of knowledge about the disorder and its treatment. Also, mental health services are taboo in the hood.

This is where the church comes in. Many urban dwellers have at least a marginal knowledge of church, perhaps in their childhoods or through neighborhood outreach events. Welcoming urban sufferers of PTSD— young and old, male and female—can become one way to reach out in the community.

TAKE IT HOME

This section is not meant to be a how-to on treating PTSD or a primer on establishing a PTSD outreach in your community. It is, however, a first step in reaching into an urban community and gang world often touched by this devastating disorder. If you are considering ways to reach into the community and, specifically, to reach urban youth, walk through these steps:

1. Prayerfully consider where God is leading, most especially in the area of PTSD services. Enough emphasis cannot be put on prayer.

2. Assess your ministry's long-term and short-term goals. Does a PTSD-related outreach fit those goals?

3. Consider your human resources: Do you have people interested in such a ministry? Are they equipped with appropriate training, or willing to become equipped?

4. Consider your physical resources: Do you have building space appropriate for such a ministry? Do you have necessary funding?

5. Assess the need: Does your congregation or your neighborhood have a need for such an outreach? Are you regularly seeing folks who could use such services?

6. Assess the mental health resources in your area for access and availability. Are there places you can recommend for those with more difficult PTSD? Will you have access to those facilities for emergencies?

7. Build relationships with mental health professionals and facilities. PTSD is a serious problem and should be treated by professionals. Those professionals must know about what you plan to do and how they can help.

8. Create ancillary services to help those suffering from PTSD, which can include transportation to accredited facilities, hotline information, print materials on the subject, even food and clothing.

There are many resources on PTSD, including books, articles, and websites. Here are several to start with:

- Sidran Traumatic Stress Institute—www.sidran.org
- National Institute of Mental Health, a subsidiary of the National Institutes of Health—www.nimh.nih.gov
- Mayo Clinic—www.mayoclinic.com
- Department of Veterans Affairs—www.ptsd.va.gov
- Intensive Trauma Therapy—www.traumatherapy.us
- *In Living Color: An Intercultural Approach to Pastoral Care and Counseling* by Emmanuel Y. Lartey
- *Pastoral Care for Post-Traumatic Stress Disorder: Healing the Shattered Soul* by Dalene Fuller Rogers
- *Post-Traumatic Stress Disorder for Dummies* by Mark Goulston
- *The Post-Traumatic Stress Disorder Sourcebook: A Guide to Healing, Recovery, and Growth* by Glenn Schiraldi
- *The PTSD Workbook: Simple, Effective Techniques for Overcoming Traumatic Stress Symptoms* by Mary Beth Williams and Soili Poijula

INTO SALVATION

God uses circumstances and his people to redeem from the edge.

My return to Grand Rapids meant one thing—a visit with the General. I knew I could be severely hurt at a minimum by the gang, so making peace was top priority. I wasn't sure peace was possible, but I knew I had to try if I had any chance of survival.

At 5:55 p.m. on Friday, I walked into the house where I'd lived for years and the gang held its meetings. It was like a ghost walked in the room. Everyone froze, unable to move and not knowing what to do or say. In some ways, I was a ghost. I was someone the new guys had only heard of, with stories good and bad. They didn't know whether to ask my advice or kill me on the spot.

The General spoke first: "What do you have to say for yourself, Bat?"

I gave him my story, telling him and the gang that I felt my crew had been in great danger and that most of the brothers had done nothing. We had been fighting a war on Francis Street that we could not win. I expressed my displeasure and feelings of betrayal.

I stood in the raw silence, waiting for the verdict. We all watched, hardly daring to breathe. The next seconds could mean the beat-down of my life, or worse; those seconds could also offer reprieve. The General stared at me, balled his fist, and dismissed me with just a wave. His gesture meant I could live, but I couldn't live in Grand Rapids anymore.

> I whirled around and ran as fast as I could away from that house. I ran and ran, away from my past and toward my future.

I nodded, not daring to utter a word as I backed inch by inch out of the room. I felt like I was trying to escape the attack of a wild animal. Once I was out of sight of the bangers, though, I whirled around and ran as fast as I could away from that house. I ran and ran, away from my past and toward my future.

FLEE IN FEAR

Despite my discharge from the gang, I was still skittish about visiting area clubs. I shouldn't have been there anyway, seeing as I was trying to escape my past life of crime, and I was supposed to be out of the city. But old habits die hard—there were people to meet, music to hear, girls to flirt with, and dancing to do. I could hardly know that one of my visits to the club SoSo's would change my life once again. I met a girl there one night.

There was something about LaDawn Thomas that drew me in. She looked good and seemed to have her act together. I saw her from across the bar, then called my little brother over so that I could play the big man. I handed him a flyer and had him take it to her. It was an invitation to an after-hours get-together. She smiled at me from across the room, and I knew I had her on the line. She met me at the party, where we danced like crazy. We exchanged phone numbers before she headed back to Detroit. Calls went back and forth, messages were left. She visited Grand Rapids several more times, and we were able to connect.

I decided that LaDawn was my ticket out of Grand Rapids. I was restless, didn't have any real work, maybe a bit depressed as I came to terms with my past life and thought about not knowing what my life would look like in the future. I didn't have any plans, not to mention job skills, but Detroit and LaDawn seemed like a good option.

So I packed my little burgundy bag once again and this time I headed east. I was used to the big city of Atlanta, so Detroit didn't seem so bad. And it wasn't. LaDawn lived in a little bungalow; it was so quiet and clean that I wandered around in wonder for days. I found peace at her home, which released something within me that was akin to a detox situation. I would jar awake in the night with my fists clenched and sweating; I sat in the dark for hours drinking myself into a stupor. I was withdrawn and quiet, not my usual MO, that's for sure. I truly felt that no one could understand me.

Looking back now, I realize I was grieving my past life with its violence and crime and in recovery from the trauma of my gang experiences. Whatever it was, I needed to be away, sit in solitude, and heal. LaDawn knew nothing of my past life, but

> It was almost like I needed to go through the steps of maturity for the first time, from learning how to carry on a conversation that didn't involve threats and foul language, to hanging out with people without fear for my life.

accepted me for who I was at that moment. Part of my healing was her daughter Adrienne, then 3, who was a bit spoiled and did not want anyone to get close to her mama. As I spent more time with them, I quickly grew to love both LaDawn and Adrienne as they helped me look outside myself and begin to reenter the world.

I started to come back to civilian life bit by bit. (Gang life is remarkably similar to military life; it just lacks adherence to the law.) I'd go out to clubs once in a while, making an attempt to be an adult. I had to learn these skills slowly, having jumped right from childhood into gang life and its dangers and craziness. It was almost like I needed to go through the steps of maturity for the first time, from learning how to carry on a conversation that didn't involve threats and foul language, to hanging out with people without fear for my life.

LaDawn was working in the corporate world and going to college, a world I knew nothing about. Once again, I was unsure of where I fit.

INTO THE ARMS

My body threw me into a tailspin one spring evening just before Easter 1994. I was the guy who could drink two cases of beer and not even stumble. I had consumed more cheap alcohol than most by that point, but that night just two beers had me sloppy drunk and wandering all over the place. LaDawn's cousin and her boyfriend didn't know what to make of it, and neither did I. Why, after all this time, couldn't I drink even two beers?

> Church became to me the white man's trick to keep black folks enslaved; it became a proponent of institutional racism, a gimmick ruled by a code book written by men who had a vested interest in keeping black folks under their thumbs.

God, of course. He was preparing me for another step in my journey. I woke up the next morning not wanting to drink. I drank anyway that weekend, but I wasn't into it. It's almost as if God started taking the desire away like he had taken away the will to fight all those months ago.

LaDawn, who by that time had stopped drinking with me altogether, invited me to church that Easter weekend. My attitude toward church had a few kinks, to say the least. My childhood experiences twisted my mind to think that church people didn't care about the real me, only about appearances and behavior. I thought they were judgmental and hypocritical, not living out what they were saying. The same cats who sat in church on Sunday morning back in Grand Rapids were drinking and using foul language just like me the next day. I couldn't understand a word those preachers were saying anyway.

My attitude matured as I did. Church became to me the white man's trick to keep black folks enslaved; it became a proponent of institutional racism, a gimmick ruled by a code book written by men who had a vested interest in keeping black folks under their thumbs.

But hey, I liked LaDawn, and everyone goes to church on Easter. Holiday church attendance is a given in the black community, whether it's Christmas, Easter, or the Fourth of July. So I threw on the only clothes I had and was ready to go to church. LaDawn and I were among thousands who attended Word of Faith International Christian Center that day in Redford, Michigan.

This multicultural, multigenerational church drew me though my attendance was still limited to holidays. There aren't that many between Easter and mid-June, but I was there on Father's Day.

"I do not belong here," I said to myself. "I don't look like the other folks (my banger wardrobe had not yet evolved), and I don't smell like other folks (after my bout with drinking the night before)." But attend I did, getting lost in the crowd but discovering that maybe church wasn't so bad after all. There were dudes willing to hug me! I probably shook fifteen to twenty people's hands before I sat down.

This multicultural, multigenerational church drew me though my attendance was still limited to holidays. There aren't that many between Easter and mid-June, but I was there on Father's Day.

Renowned gospel singer Helen Baylor was rocking the house as she called people to worship. I could certainly appreciate Baylor's story, with her rise to fame from the streets of Compton, Los Angeles, to the top of the Christian music charts. She started her career in nightclubs, eventually opening for Aretha Franklin, B. B. King, and Stevie Wonder. Her descent into drug abuse derailed her career, but she got sober and found God once again. This was a woman I could understand.

I was expecting Bishop Keith Butler—pastor of Word of Faith—to speak that morning, but instead he introduced the guest speaker, evangelist Jessie

DuPlantis. Me, the racist, listen to a middle-aged white preacher? I was twitching in my seat.

But when Jessie opened his mouth, I couldn't help but listen. He was hilarious, but he was also explaining the Word of God in a way I could understand. "It's not enough to be a man," he said. "You have to stand up and be God's man!"

> "Take all this stuff from me," I prayed, kneeling at the front of the church. "Take away my taste for violence, womanizing attitude, and bad language. If you're real, God, take it away from me."

To my utter surprise, my heart began to move. God touched me that Father's Day morning. When Jessie called worshipers to make a decision, I was standing up and walking down that aisle faster than I thought possible.

"Take all this stuff from me," I prayed, kneeling at the front of the church. "Take away my taste for violence, my womanizing attitude, bad language. If you're real, God, take it away from me."

He did. God came into my life and started working on me immediately through his love. LaDawn had given her life back to Christ that morning as well, so we began to grow together. Five months later we were married and still are today, more than fifteen years later.

I look to that Sunday morning as the watershed in my life. My past was wiped away, my future given to God. Hope was kindled, despair destroyed. Life, not death, held sway in my world.

We attended Word of Faith for some time after our conversions, participating in small groups and other ministries. But God wasn't done with his plans for me. I felt God calling me back to the hood, back to the urban culture I'd so recently fled. Back to my people, bangers, drug users and sellers, to the kinds of neighborhoods I'd once ruled with guns and threats. This time I wanted to come with hope and love.

TAKE IT HOME

God has blessed me in that I have seen thousands of lives saved through others' and my own ministry. I've witnessed people young and old, black, white, and Hispanic give their lives to Jesus and come away changed.

One young woman from the inner city practiced witchcraft but still hung around our church with a group of teens. She wasn't interested in "churchy stuff," but she was very interested in the fellowship these kids had to offer.

One day the teens were outside my office at our first church plant; they were listening to music and laughing, just having a good time together. The mood shifted as they started getting into worship music, and I could hear the kids sharing their stories of coming to Christ. After a bit, someone began to cry, and soon the group brought the young lady into my office.

I spoke to her, and in two minutes that young lady went from being a practicing witch to a child of God. The key was talking to her in language she could understand instead of using churchy, theological, and academic words.

Though I was excited about leading this young lady to Christ, I was equally disappointed with myself that we had not prepared our youth, or the church for that matter, to lead anyone to Jesus. In the urban setting, it is crucial that we educate the church body on how to lead someone to Christ. As I travel across the country, I'm always startled at how many people don't know how. Here are several suggestions.

1. Raise the individual soul-winning temperature.

- Encourage Christ-centered fellowship among peer groups, which will encourage authentic relationships that form the basis for leading others to Christ.
- Teach from the pulpit that the entire body of Christ is responsible for sharing Jesus, not just the pastor. Many people don't feel they

are called to help win souls; they are waiting for their spiritual leader to tell them they are.

- Just do it. Talk to people, share your faith, and see what God will do.

2. Give individuals the tools to lead people to Christ. Here is an easy acronym—the ABCs of salvation—to help explain salvation and teach people how to win souls:

- A—Admit you are a sinner. "There is no one righteous, not even one . . . for all have sinned and fall short of the glory of God" (Rom. 3:10, 23; see also Rom. 5:8; 6:23).
- A—Ask God's forgiveness. "Everyone who calls on the name of the Lord will be saved" (Rom. 10:13).
- B—Believe in Jesus (put your trust in him) as your only hope of salvation. "For God so loved the world that he gave his one and only Son, that whoever believes in him shall not perish but have eternal life" (John 3:16; see also John 14:6).
- B—Become a child of God by receiving Christ. "To all who receive him, to those who believed in his name, he gave the right to become children of God" (John 1:12; see also Rev. 3:20).
- C—Confess that Jesus is your Lord. "If you confess with your mouth, 'Jesus is Lord,' and believe in your heart that God raised him from the dead, you will be saved" (Rom. 10:9).

One of my favorite messages to the church is about Ananias, an early and devout follower of Jesus. He was given special instructions by God to go find Saul of Tarsus. Saul was a Pharisee and a dangerous persecutor of all Christ-followers.

I often refer to Saul as a banger among bangers. Sounds a bit crazy calling a first-century Jew a gangbanger; but if you think about it, he represented the Jews, who came against anyone who called themselves Christians. That sure sounds like gang rivalry to me.

Saul was on his way to Damascus to further his persecution of Jesus' followers there, until he met Jesus himself on that dusty road. Saul recognized Christ and was immediately blinded. He praised Jesus even in his new blindness, then headed to Damascus to pray and wait. Ananias was told by God to find Saul in Damascus and speak life to him. Here is Ananias' response, found in Acts 9: "'Lord,' Ananias answered, 'I have heard many reports about this man and all the harm he has done to your saints in Jerusalem. And he has come here with authority from the chief priests to arrest all who call on your name'" (vv. 13–14).

Ananias responded like we all would have—pointing out Saul's reputation as a persecutor of Christians. Obviously fear filled his heart, just as fear fills our hearts when we are asked to share our faith. Sometimes sharing Jesus is not a comfortable thing to do. "But the Lord said to Ananias, 'Go! This man is my chosen instrument to carry my name before the Gentiles and their kings and before the people of Israel. I will show him how much he must suffer for my name'" (vv. 15–16).

God didn't merely suggest that Ananias go; God ordered Ananias to go, just as he orders us to go and share our faith. God had already prepared Saul's heart for the calling on his life, just as he prepares those with whom we share. "Then Ananias went to the house and entered it. Placing his hands on Saul, he said, 'Brother Saul, the Lord—Jesus, who appeared to you on the road as you were coming here—has sent me that you may see again and be filled with the Holy Spirit'" (v. 17).

Ananias was willing to confirm with Saul his calling, as well as share the good news of Christ with him. "Immediately, something like scales fell from Saul's eyes, and he could see again. He got up and was baptized, and after taking some food, he regained his strength. . . . At once he began to preach in the synagogues that Jesus is the Son of God" (vv. 18–20).

Imagine if Ananias had not shared the gospel and missed out on the opportunity to pour into Paul's life. We must not miss our opportunity to pour into someone who could be the next apostle Paul. To do so in the urban context requires several special considerations:

1. Build Relationships. Try to build a relationship with the person you hope to lead to Christ. Urban youth and adults are wary of people pushing into their faces with any message; they are much more willing to listen to someone they know and who knows them.

2. Do not Assume Anything. Just because a person is poor doesn't mean he or she doesn't know Jesus. Be willing to ask about and then listen to anyone's spiritual journey and life story.

3. Take responsibility for Sharing the Gospel. The person you want to see follow Christ shouldn't have to ask; you should open the door and be willing to tell. My friend Pastor Paul Hontz says to open your conversations with, "Has anyone ever taken the time to share with you what the Bible says about being born again?" This takes the responsibility off the person and puts it on the body of Christ and individual believers.

PART 4

THE CHURCH

16

TRANSFORMED TO SERVE

We must build skills in the "outcast" to affirm his or her dignity.

LaDawn and I found a church home at Rose of Sharon Church of God in Christ (we called it "the Rose"), a small urban church in Detroit pastored by Ronald L. Griffin. Pastor Griffin was from Buffalo, New York, and had left his street background to become a successful businessman. He was president of the Detroit Urban League for awhile before devoting his life to saving souls on the streets of Detroit.

He was one radical dude who gathered an army of young cats in their early twenties who were ready to take on the world for Christ. They were fighting God's war with tactics I understood. He took a bunch of guys off the streets, some just released from jail or from the block where the church was located, and lit them on fire for the Lord.

> His was a faith that extended into the streets and lives of the most vulnerable and downtrodden, the most hardened bangers and criminals. The past didn't matter . . . only where a person's heart stood with God.

Pastor Griffin taught radical worship and radical service. His was a faith that extended into the streets and lives of the most vulnerable and downtrodden, the most hardened bangers and criminals. The past didn't matter to Pastor Griffin, only where a person's heart stood with God.

This out-of-the-box pastor gave me a fresh, imaginative look at how church could be. I loved everything about the Rose, serving others, and growing in Christ. I was there four to five nights a week working in the church and serving young people. (That's churchy talk for spending time with kids who often didn't have a place to go, buying them food, laughing, listening to music, and just being an adult they could count on.)

> I fell in love with the English language for the first time, a clear miracle for the kid who dropped out of school with second-grade reading skills.
> I soaked up every book I could find, but mostly the Bible.

That ministry blew up—in a good way. My good friend Robert Bush taught me everything about serving youth and serving in general. We worked together to build the youth ministry from scratch. It was hard-core relational, doing life on life with these kids literally at street level. Bush didn't just reach out to kids; he reached out to me, too, being one of the first of my peers to really pour into me in the area of ministry.

My brother in the Lord, KaShawn Akins, began leading me through biblical principles, diving with me into the Word of God. And through reading the Bible, he taught me to read. I fell in love with the English language for the first time, a clear miracle for the kid who dropped out of school with second-grade reading skills. I soaked up every book I could find, but mostly the Bible. I drew from its life-giving words.

SPIRITUALLY EMPLOYED

While my spiritual life flourished on a number of fronts, I also needed a job. Seeing as job skills weren't top on my priority list during my banger days, I had limited options. But I had big dreams! I was working in a factory—back when Detroit had factory jobs to spare—when I saw a technician come in and start working on the computers.

"I'm going to do that job someday," I bragged to my buddies on the line. Immediately they dared me to try it. Never one to back down from a dare, I started praying. And God started sending people into my life who had knowledge of computers.

One of the first was ACE, which stands for All Created Equal. His real name is Corey Turner, and he had banged with me in Grand Rapids for awhile before moving back to Detroit and getting his life together.

ACE began helping me achieve my computer dreams by reading manuals to me every night, explaining stuff as we went along. He was a trained Novell certified engineer, a job I aspired to as well. While ACE trained me on computer stuff, KaShawn taught me how to interview for tech positions and how to take tests. I actually passed a test that allowed me to become a Novell certified administrator, which led to a job working on the national tech team help desk.

As I look back now, I see God's hand in every moment of this time in my life. Only a miracle can explain how a former banger with two felony convictions and low reading skills could become a computer technician, then a network administrator, then a technical engineer, and finally move into management. For the first time in my life, I was a productive member of society and actually had a little money to spend.

> Only a miracle can explain how a former banger with two felony convictions and low reading skills could become a computer technician, then a network administrator, then a technical engineer, and finally move into management.

I worked on a team that developed UPS online software, obtained certifications in about a dozen technology-related things, including the prestigious Microsoft platform, and ended up working in technology for General Motors, the Bing Group, NBD Bank, and Highland Park School District. God was truly being glorified in the midst of what I was doing.

One of my greatest learning experiences came when God introduced me to Andrew Wallace. Andrew, a former marijuana dealer and mechanic, had opened his own computer business. He made his first million from his dining room table; in recent years, he has earned twelve million dollars.

> His business was about ministry, about touching others for Christ. While he ran his technology business well, for him the real goal was being a blessing to others.

I had lost my lucrative job with the Bing Group, during which I had been working with Andrew on the side. He hired me full time but then fired me and gave me a hundred dollars to start my own business. Andrew knew exactly what he was doing. He hired me and my new company back, as well as contracted me out to a number of places.

Andrew wasn't just teaching me about running a business and information technology; he was teaching me how to become a blessing to others. He loved to interview prospective employees and, when he found their interview skills lacking, give them sound advice and tell them to come back tomorrow. He hired a homeless woman who was living in her car; he hired a girl some might have thought was learning disabled but who only needed an opportunity and a chance.

His business was about ministry, about touching others for Christ. While he ran his technology business well, for him the real goal was being a blessing to others. "Want to be part of a blessing?" he'd say as he walked by my office. I knew this meant he'd found someone who needed help and thought I'd like to be part of whatever he was about to do.

There was an incident at the *Chicago Tribune* that I'll always remember. We were there making a presentation to the company in the hopes of landing a contract. As we sat in the meeting full of people, Andrew suddenly said, "Can we pray?" Nobody disagreed, so he began to pray. Pretty soon there were people crying and praying as well. Andrew had changed the dynamic of that meeting into an opportunity to bless others and influence their lives for Christ. His drive to take every opportunity to advance the kingdom of God still influences me today.

My technology training provided me with job opportunities I couldn't have imagined just a few years before; my spiritual training deepened and broadened my love for God and others. And it changed my life direction once again. LaDawn and I added to our family, first Toni in 1997, and then Erin in 2000. LaDawn cared for them at home, as well as staying heavily involved at the Rose.

I enjoyed technology, but I loved God more. I first heeded his call to work in ministry at the church, then listened once again. He called me to leave my lucrative career and become a pastor. God was calling me back to Grand Rapids.

THE REDEMPTION OF SERVING

The idea that I was usable was a big deal. I'd been nothing but a drain on society for so long that I didn't know any other way. But even the apostle Paul (my favorite New Testament banger) started sharing Christ immediately.

I'm not suggesting that we put new Christians on the soul-winning front lines immediately; I am suggesting that we get them involved in meaningful service quickly. When everything a person knows about him- or herself has been stripped away by the Holy Spirit, it's easy to feel worthless and unusable. It's easy to think that God couldn't possibly use such a wounded soul. But using wounded souls is God's specialty.

Many who have left street life look for opportunities to serve and give back to the very communities they helped poison. The church is indeed the light and hope of the world, as well as a viable and important source for lasting social and spiritual change.

I believe we—you, me, and the church—must create opportunities for men and women whose lives have been changed by God to make a difference in their communities. They must know that, despite their rough edges, their communities, churches, and families value and need them.

TAKE IT HOME

Our goal must be to encourage others in the faith even as we encourage them to become productive, assimilated members of the community. All of us are God's creation, all of us have gifts, and all of us can show love to one another. Check out these examples of love in action.

- Homeboy Industries started in Los Angeles as Jobs for a Future, a program created by Father Gregory Boyle to offer job training and other help to those who wanted an alternative to gang life. The program offers jobs to hard-to-place bangers that teach them skills needed in the outside world. Homeboy Industries became an independent nonprofit in 2001. Former gang members can build a résumé and gain work experience at the Homeboy Bakery; Homegirl Café and Catering; Homeboy Maintenance, Merchandise, Silkscreen & Embroidery; and Homeboy Press. One unique service they offer is tattoo removal, where a team of volunteer physicians and assistants perform about five thousand treatments a year (www.homeboy-industries.org).
- Lawndale Community Church in Chicago has been involved in community outreach for years, with programs such as Lawndale Christian Development Corporation, Lawndale Christian Health Center, and Lawndale Christian Legal Center. The church began working with Lou Malnati's, one of the most famous pizzerias in Chicago, to offer a place for former drug addicts and ex-cons to reenter the work world. Malnati's opened a pizzeria in Lawndale, committing to reinvesting their profits into the community and hiring residents of the church's rehabilitation center.

- At The EDGE Christian Fellowship in Grand Rapids, we are committed to hiring youth and young adults from our urban area to serve in meaningful roles in the ministry. We have a member who offers help to teenage men and women from the hood as they seek to reenter regular society. These kids have learned client relations, invoicing, marketing, and other job skills, as well as training such as interviewing techniques. Imagine the impact on an eighteen-year-old to provide marketing services for several well-known gospel artists, a seventeen-year-old dancer from the inner city being coached through opening a Christian dance company, or a young man from Detroit being trained as a network technician. This is the hope we, the church, pursue.

Urban churches can offer an invaluable resource for at-risk youth, former gang members, and those wanting to leave the gang. Providing job and life skills is one of the best ways to return bangers to responsible life while allowing them to maintain their dignity.

17

CONTINUING STRUGGLE

The redeemed must know the heavy weight of discrimination.

God was calling me back to Grand Rapids to repair what I had broken, as well as pour back into the community all I had taken out. LaDawn and I immediately began to pray, and together made the decision that Grand Rapids would become our new home.

I wish I could say this was a seamless journey, but it was a struggle to make the transition. My friends and church home were all in Detroit. The city represented a new life and a new start for me. Detroit was where I became a new man in Christ, but also where I learned to be a real man. Pastor Griffin, Andrew Wallace, Robert Bush, KaShawn Akins, Corey Turner—these were all men who had poured their lives into me, and I would miss their friendship and example. I felt like I owed them all so much.

There was another dimension to my ambivalence about returning to Grand Rapids. Frankly, I was afraid of the unknown; I didn't know how people would receive me when I returned to my old neighborhood. The last time I had been in the city I was a "dead man walking." I had done so much dirt that I had enemies I didn't even know about.

Before I left, during the Francis Street Mob days, I had taken drugs from several big-time dealers and dared them to say something about it. I had hurt so many women that I couldn't even keep count. I had left my family without thinking twice about it. I had a strained relationship with my son Anthony despite having him for most holidays, during the summer, and during visits to Grand Rapids. I tried to explain to him that I had to live away from Grand Rapids to avoid risking both of our lives because of my past. But in his ten-year-old mind, I had abandoned him.

> The yearning I felt was stronger than my fear. . . . I was thoroughly convinced of God's call.

Though I had been married to LaDawn for four years at this point, I had not shared with her the level of my involvement in the street life and gang. I knew the day would come—sooner rather than later—that I would have to share my darkest secrets that so far had remained buried. Returning to Grand Rapids meant I would need to face my past and the fears and dangers associated with it.

But the yearning I felt was stronger than my fear. I dreamed about the move and talked about it often. I was thoroughly convinced of God's call that I reach the urban culture back in Grand Rapids.

THE POWER OF HUMILITY

Because of strict guidelines of the Church of God in Christ regarding church plants, I wasn't sure how Pastor Griffin would respond to my strong desire to plant a church. We decided to get the legwork done first, moving forward initially without letting the denomination know. For six months, my family weekly drove the two hours to Grand Rapids to build a core group of believers that would help launch the church.

When I finally spoke to Pastor Griffin about this calling and how I had been going to Grand Rapids to prepare, he gave me his blessing and vowed to be available with advice as needed.

In December 2000, LaDawn, Adrienne, Toni, Erin (still an infant), and I moved to Grand Rapids. After months of communication, meetings in homes, and promotion, we launched Knowledge of Truth Church of God in Christ with roughly one hundred people in attendance. We held services at Holiday Inn in the heart of downtown Grand Rapids. I was a twenty-five-year-old preacher ready to take on the world without a clue how to do it. I had no financial support and none of the training I needed and desired.

Of course the inevitable occurred unexpectedly. I was on my way to my brother's home in a low-income housing complex just outside of town. I was taking life easy, driving along listening to music when, out of the corner of my eye, I saw the General. I would know his walk anywhere. I stomped on the brakes, jammed the car in reverse, and backed into a parking place. I jumped from the car without thinking or attempting to come up with an explanation of why I was back in the area after being told—by him—not to be.

He turned and looked at me, then beckoned me to follow him toward his apartment. I walked in as he closed the door behind me.

> My life was no longer forfeit, given back to me by a powerful gang leader who had once been like an uncle to me.

"I heard you was doing the church thing," he said.

"Yes, sir," was all I could say. My life hung in the balance in so many ways at the moment. But the tension eased.

The General told me I was looking good and that he loved me.

He reached out and shook my hand without using the gang handshake.

"All is well," he said.

My heart started beating once again.

"All is well" is code for saying I was cool. My life was no longer forfeit, given back to me by a powerful gang leader who had once been like an uncle to me.

I made to leave, which he allowed, telling me not to reveal where he lived. That brief encounter was the last time I saw the General. He died unexpectedly several years later.

> With God's help, I was able to extend the same grace to him that had been extended to me by the General and most importantly by the Lord.

Another inevitable encounter occurred several months after our move. I was pumping gas at a station in the city when I looked across to the other pump. There, oblivious to me, was the dude who had shot my brother Mark. This was another moment of testing, a second when I could make a life-giving or a life-sapping choice. I could simply drive away; I could confront him and demand retribution; I could show him the love of Jesus. I wish I could say I didn't contemplate the worst choice.

My heart raced as the gas pump clicked. Almost instinctively, I walked toward him. Needless to say, his eyes about came out of his face when he saw me.

"I'm not sure if you know, but I'm a pastor now," I said as I stuck my hand out to him.

"I heard," he replied.

I looked straight at him, took a deep breath, swallowed my pride, and said, "We are straight."

With God's help, I was able to extend the same grace to him that had been extended to me by the General and most importantly by the Lord.

After being in ministry for a year with no pay, LaDawn and I decided that I should get a job. I applied and interviewed for technology jobs for which I was more than qualified, often the only black person interviewing for these high-end positions. But I could see a prospective employer's face drop when I entered the room.

This is a rare feeling—watching someone express disappointment at who you are. If I wasn't treated differently because of the color of my skin, I was refused employment because of my felony record. Even with my years of experience, those convictions made getting a job difficult. It became so difficult that LaDawn had to find a job after years of being at home with our children. This reality sent me into a deep depression, which I refused to discuss with anyone. I would often preach with nothing in my soul, or cancel the service altogether.

I finally did find a hustle: selling BBQ chicken on a street corner and taking pictures for people with an old 35mm camera I borrowed from my dad. God taught me all about humility, but he also put me in a place where the community came to know me. I was back on the street, this time hawking chicken instead of drugs and sharing the true gospel with anyone who would listen.

THE CALL OF A LIFETIME

Only after I learned that important lesson in humility did God begin to work out my situation. I was asked to interview with the American Red Cross as their information technology person and, as usual, I was the only person of color in the room. The local American Red Cross chapter had only two African-American employees in the history of the chapter, so when I was asked to return for a third interview, I simply waited for the shoe to drop.

> Only after I learned that important lesson in humility did God begin to work out my situation.

"I see that you have a felony for selling drugs," the CEO stated. "You don't look like a person who would sell drugs."

"Ma'am, in the early 1990s, people in my hood sold drugs like a hobby. Kids would get involved selling drugs like the kids in your hood would sign up for the baseball team." I was able to share my God story with her and the team.

She hired me for the position, and I loved every minute of that job.

I worked for the American Red Cross and pastored Knowledge of Truth. Several years into the work, we changed our name to the nondenominational Christ-Like Outreach Ministries. Those eight years as senior pastor were good years, difficult at times but a huge learning experience and an opportunity to see God at work in lives.

But I started to sense that God wanted me to do more. So many young people were getting shot, beat up, arrested—so many were involved in the gang life with its emphasis on crime. The church seemed uninterested in reaching this culture. We were good at reaching the homeless and even drug addicts, but not too many ministries were open to receiving and loving a practicing gang member. Sitting in my air-conditioned office at the Red Cross, I wept week after week as I increasingly ached for the souls all around me, struggling in their own living hells.

> The church seemed uninterested in reaching this culture. We were good at reaching the homeless and even drug addicts, but not too many ministries were open to receiving and loving a practicing gang member.

My dream of reaching out to gang members came closer to reality when my new nonprofit Strategic Outreach Services sponsored a citywide conference on gangs. LaDawn left her prosperous career in fund development to do promotion for the event, which drew church leaders, law enforcement personnel, educators, city officials, and gang members. We worked on these conferences for about six months before I felt the Lord telling me that he needed more.

We closed Christ-Like Outreach so I could dedicate more of my time to reaching out to gang members. It was painful to close this ministry, but we knew we must move on to what God had next for us.

For years I had attended the Urban Youth Workers Institute in California, and 2006 was no exception. For the first time, LaDawn was able to attend with me. The conference, designed to encourage and equip urban youth workers, draws thousands of people from all walks of life with a common dream—bringing urban youth to Christ.

Dr. Larry Acosta, founder of UYWI, gave the closing message that year. "Some of you are looking for the next thing to do in your ministry," he said. "Stop looking to excel in the mainstream church and consider whether God is calling you to commit to urban ministry for a lifetime."

LaDawn and I both began to cry, and that night we decided to embrace the call of a lifetime.

CLOSER TOWARD UNITY

The church must understand that the color of a person's skin can be a barrier to so many things. I don't want to offend, but I do want people to understand that many people of color feel that their skin color is a permanent stumbling block to success.

I experienced this feeling when I didn't get past a first job interview because I was black, or I didn't get jobs because I was a felon. I was looked down on because of the color of my skin or choice of clothes.

Equally frustrating is the fact that many of my white brothers and sisters will never experience what I'm describing. I took a course called Healing Racism (at a Grand Rapids church offering the training), during which we participated in a round-table discussion. The curriculum and teacher did a good job explaining what white privilege looks like in the areas of housing, education, employment, and so forth. Yet I was completely thrown off trying to discuss with an all-white group of Christians about the privileges they have. Several exercises made clear that those privileges were indeed reality, but I was still perplexed by their response of "I really did not know."

> Stop looking to excel in the mainstream church and consider whether God is calling you to commit to urban ministry for a lifetime.

"How can they not know about the privileges they have?" I asked myself.

The next day I talked to a Christian brother at work about the class and my frustration with the white brothers and sisters not realizing how much they have.

"Troy, how can we be aware that something is a privilege when we've never had to live without it?" my friend asked.

The light came on. Unless you wear dark skin every day, you'll never experience the pain and heaviness that comes with it. I asked him, a white man, if he'd ever experienced any of these things strictly because of the color of his skin:

> How can we be aware that something is a privilege when we've never had to live without it?

- Not being hired for a job.
- Wearing Sunday best to a casual meeting because you don't want to be stereotyped.
- Avoiding naming your children African or unique names because you don't want colleges or employers to know they're black before they are even given a chance.
- Keeping your hands out of your pockets in a store because you don't want to be accused of stealing.
- Being pulled over by a police officer, but not knowing why.
- Being asked by a store clerk if you need help because you've been looking around too long.
- Observing people locking their car doors when you walk by.

The truth is that many young African-Americans feel imprisoned by the color of their skin, which makes it difficult to excel outside of what society expects of them. The church, both black and white, must gain perspective on the weight felt by so many brothers and sisters of color. Awareness will save many misunderstandings as we intentionally move closer toward Christian unity.

TAKE IT HOME

I wrote this little expressive essay several years ago while working in corporate America. I felt the pain of always being in my dark skin, my own prison, and yearned to escape. My hope is that it sheds light on the feelings of many in the urban setting.

My Prison—My Skin—My Escape

Before my conception, I was labeled guilty of the ultimate crime.

In my innocence . . . I . . . was convicted . . . and upon my birth, I was sentenced to serve my time. Hauled off into a prison that I cannot escape.

Now in youth detention, I am serving my time, not quite understanding all that is going on, but the reality is . . . that it is . . . something going on. It was not until my teenage years that I knew that I was in prison.

It was made known to me by those outside the walls but reinforced by those inside the prison with me. . . . They categorized; they picked at you; they decided who looked the best, who was the norm, who had the best hair. But they failed to realize that they were, too, in their own 6x9 cell. . . . Those with lighter uniforms became so consumed with ensuring that those with the darker uniforms knew they were not the same, that they forgot that they too were in their prison—their skin.

I graduated to the big house and the rules changed. . . . I was now fighting for my life and my newly born son, who had just entered into youth detention to serve his time . . . his skin—his prison.

I learned the game and the tricks fitting for an individual of my caliber. . . . I learned the hustle. . . . I needed to survive. . . . I needed to show the other inmates that I was not going to be raped, abused, and mistreated. . . . My popularity became my claim to fame, a coward hiding behind my reputation and ability to do great bodily harm.

But hey . . . this is the name of the game. . . . Shank or get shanked. . . . Those on the outside and the guards who patrolled and watched as we participated in this animal-like behavior . . . I observed the Chaplain and the older prisoners not saying much . . . but they would shake their heads in great disgust . . . I am not sure if it's my fault or theirs, but it's a reality.

I decide to give myself to a female inmate who can only partially understand what it is to be a male inmate. . . . So my additional abuse that caused me great confusion, anger, and frustration because I am a male inmate, she would not ever fully understand or experience . . . hmmmm . . . division . . . at its best. Shortly after I have three daughters in their prisons—their skins.

After serving twenty-five years, I was released with a lifetime parole. . . . You know, I gathered some education, changed my diction, stopped participating in the hustle . . . I became a business owner, but still . . . sentenced to life on tether. We tried to deny the tether . . . but little did I know, from my conception, a security feature was made a part of me and the system knew that I could not escape it. . . . As soon as I "get out of my place" I am reminded that I am still a prisoner . . . you know . . . when you go to the store . . . go to work . . . get an interview . . . get pulled over by the police . . . out in the suburbs and stop to get directions . . . pumping gas . . . fancy restaurants . . . you are being watched, judged, and profiled . . . but hey, this is my sentence.

The thing most confusing is that those who are not imprisoned do not see my bars. They seem to think that because we are in the twentieth century that prisons are not real. . . . See, they can move along freely with no chains and be accepted. But me, I am sentenced for life to my prison—my skin.

PS: I forgot to mention . . . all is not lost. . . . I do have a hope which is in Christ Jesus . . . and that hope is, one day I will be caught up in the air to meet my Father. He will look at me and I will be judged by my decision to accept his Son and his ways and not by the color of my skin. Finally I will be made a free man throughout eternity . . . my escape.

APPROACHING THE EDGE

Loving neighbors requires being in the neighborhood.

We sat in a tree house planning what would become The EDGE Urban Fellowship. As much as we would have liked to have been in an actual tree house, LaDawn, Kenny Russell, Leonard "Street Alert" Rosses, his wife Lydia Rosses, and I sat in an indoor tree house designed for kids' small groups at Impact, a church started in Lowell, Michigan, in 2003 by Kentwood Community Church.

Kentwood Community Church (KCC, located in Kentwood, Michigan) is the parent church of The EDGE and the church my family and I attended after disbanding Christ-Like Outreach Ministries. My dream had always been to reach the urban hip-hop culture; KCC's commitment to church planting seemed like a good fit for what God was calling us to. As I got to know the heart of Wayne Schmidt (former lead pastor) and pastor Kyle Ray (now KCC's senior pastor), we began to flesh out the idea of an urban church plant.

Pastor Kyle recalls, "Troy had the passion, the relationship connections, and certainly the missionary call to the inner city. He loves the Lord and represents Jesus well in the hip-hop culture. We recognized that certain churches reach certain groups, so we knew that it would take a unique church to reach people we wouldn't normally reach."

We talked and prayed over the months, discussing whether The EDGE would be a church implant (people from KCC move to the church plant), a parachurch group, or an independent church plant. We considered offering a hip-hop service on Saturday nights at KCC (parachurch), but decided God was calling me to plant a church in the neighborhood where I once did my dirt.

FINDING THE EDGE

This development process coincided with the yearly Nitrogen conference, a gathering designed to teach and encourage those interested in planting a church using curriculum developed by Impact founding pastor Phil Struckmeyer. The three-day boot camp helps church-planting teams from around the country develop a strategy for their new endeavors. After giving us instructions for our planning session, we were sent to our tree house to brainstorm.

We were to identify our target audience, geographical location, and what the typical Ms./Mrs. and Mr. EDGE might look like. We drew a stick person in the middle of a sticky pad, then were to write down what our typical attendee looked like and what his or her needs might be.

We knew several things:

- We wanted the church to appeal to the hip-hop culture.
- A large percentage of hip-hop music is purchased by white, teenage females.
- Hip-hop dancers, called b-boys, are often Hispanic.
- Rappers are primarily young, African-American men.
- Hip-hop became popular in the 1970s.

We needed to create an environment where all felt welcome. Not an easy task, but one I relished and knew God was leading me to. The first thing we needed to do was define what it means to be an "environment" in the midst of the culture. I didn't want to plant a church because it's the cool thing to do in Christian circles. I wanted to plant a church because it's the best method to win people to Christ.

Several denominational studies have confirmed that the average new church gains most of its members (60 to 80 percent) from the ranks of people not attending any worshiping body, while churches over ten to fifteen years of age gain 80 to 90 percent of new members by transfer from other congregations.

> I didn't want to plant a church because it's thecool thing to do in Christian circles. I wanted to plant a church because it's the best method to win people to Christ.

This means that the average new congregation will bring six to eight times more new people into the life of the body of Christ than an older congregation of the same size. Peter Wagner, founder of Global Harvest Ministries and former professor of church growth at Fuller Theological Seminary, said, "Planting new churches is the most effective evangelistic method under heaven."[1]

This isn't magic; it's just that a new church is designed to reach its exact audience and demographic, while existing churches are more settled and perhaps less intent on reaching the changing world around them.

We felt called to reach a unique people group—the hip-hop culture—for Jesus. We decided our typical attendee would have some or all of the following characteristics:

- unchurched, or disillusioned with traditional church;
- urban dweller;
- represents the diversity of the urban culture;

- faces issues typical of urban living, including poverty, lack of education, inadequate housing, low job skills, gang influence; and
- looking for answers to life's questions, but eager to hear those answers in language and mediums he or she can understand.

We developed these strategic statements:

- The Vision: Create an environment, in the midst of the hip-hop culture, that promotes Christ-centered living, which will transform individuals, families, and communities into disciples of Christ.
- The Mission: Proclaim the gospel of Jesus Christ to the hip-hop culture through evangelism, discipleship, spiritual growth, and empowerment.

We also adopted a portion of the traditional church concept in that we created a central meeting place for people to congregate a minimum of once a week. We would use the church service to create a thirst for community, as well as offer a bit of the "shock factor."

Five months prior to launching The EDGE, we hosted biweekly get-togethers to share the mission and vision. We gathered about thirty people who were convinced that urban ministry is where God had called them.

FINDING OUR ENVIRONMENT

We are strategically located in the middle of an urban neighborhood several miles south of downtown Grand Rapids. Gang graffiti appeared on the building within the first month, prostitutes hung out under our awning to get out of the rain, and three blocks away is a hotel known for prostitution. Yet our church offers a clean, unique look in an area that needed love.

Graffiti appears throughout our building, but we planned this wall writing. The worship center includes an eleven-by-thirty-foot graffiti piece that says, "Christ in your hood." We placed caging with colored lights around the stage to create an ambience familiar to the hip-hop culture. A nine-foot cross with one steel gate on each side hangs in the worship center. White bandannas representing those who have given their lives to Jesus hang on the gates.

> Middle-aged blacks, whites, and Hispanics attended. Youth from all over the city were present. Prostitutes, pimps, drug dealers, and gangbangers came to hear the good news of Jesus.

To our surprise, we launched the church with over 250 people in attendance. All ages, colors, and walks of life were represented. A teenage boy walked to the Session (the name for our Saturday-evening service) with his younger brothers and cousins. Middle-aged blacks, whites, and Hispanics attended. Youth from all over the city were present. Prostitutes, pimps, drug dealers, and gangbangers came to hear the good news of Jesus. People travel as far as an hour to be part of our community. And we were, and still are, completely blown away by what God is doing.

Despite our prelaunch preparations and the successful first month of operation, we still struggled with communicating this environment we felt called to create. Our team as a whole couldn't seem to grasp what environment looked like for us as a church. Many assumed that the environment was the God-honoring and exciting church service. But the church service had only about 5 percent to do with what we as a body and community were to be about. Unfortunately, our dream wasn't easily articulated or available in bullet-pointed lists; it was something we would know when we saw it.

About a month after the launch, program director Denny Johnson and I were fleshing out many of the thoughts and ideas that ended up in this book. We started to specifically dig into the concept of environment, writing down ideas on a sticky-note pad. I attempted to articulate what I felt

God was calling The EDGE to do; Denny asked me probing questions. Then it happened.

I walked to front of the church and saw environment in action. A young, white college student was helping an inner-city black kid with his math homework. Without us doing anything except creating what we hoped was the right environment, true environment took place. We didn't set up a homework help program or an after-school homework center. We created an environment where all races and cultures could come together to live in community. We discovered that environment is both a noun and a verb—both strategic and organic.

> We discovered that environment is both a noun and a verb—both strategic and organic.

Creating this environment hasn't always been easy. We know it will be a process to change the culture of what authentic Christian community/church/environment is all about. But one by one, people are able to experience the love, accountability, and genuine community that has emerged from the God-given environment at The EDGE.

KCC felt it too. "The EDGE has stretched our folks, helping us realize that we can all worship God in different mediums," said Pastor Kyle. "The EDGE has broadened our perspective on what Christianity looks like, and breaks down the stereotypes of what a big, suburban church looks like. It's always good to stretch people evangelistically."

After the excitement of the big launch, we figured that the diversity of our group would drop drastically. Not so. After more than two years in ministry, the church is maintaining the same demographics as when we started. As I look at all ages, colors, and ethnicities united in a common cause each week, I can say from the stage, "This is what the hip-hop culture looks like!"

TAKE IT HOME

Pastor Kyle Ray offers this advice for larger churches considering church plants as a form of outreach:

1. Let the new church establish its own DNA. The church plant doesn't have to be a mini version of the parent.
2. Be available for coaching, mentoring, and questions, much like a parent/child relationship.
3. Accountability is vital, with both churches providing information and details to the other regarding finances and so forth.
4. Provide opportunities for updates to the parent congregation, sharing the vision, struggles, and successes of the church plant.
5. Trust that the church plant will figure out how to do ministry in its own setting.

The EDGE is an acronym that stands for Evangelism, Discipleship, Growth, and Empowerment. We've found it to be a powerful framework for ministry.

Evangelism

To the Jews I became like a Jew, to win the Jews. To those under the law I became like one under law (though I myself am not under the law), so as to win those under the law. To those not having the law I became like one not having the law (though I am not free from God's law but am under Christ's law), so as to win those not having the law. To the weak I became weak, to win the weak. I have become all things to all men so that by all possible means I might save some. (1 Cor. 9:20–22)

We commit to community outreach that extends beyond merely a service project for people in need:

- We desire to be a witness of Christ's love in the community by being a caring, serving church.
- We use extended acts of service and mercy, and respond to those in crisis as a catalyst for building relationships.
- We seek opportunities to proclaim the Word of God to those with whom we come in contact. St. Francis of Assisi is credited with saying, "Preach the gospel always. If necessary use words."

Proclaiming the news of Christ is not limited to simply giving out pamphlets or going door to door. It is being willing to change your barbershop, if necessary, to be a witness of the gospel of Jesus. It may mean participating in your local urban school's PTA or gang task force or organizing the senior class all-nighter.

Discipleship

"Therefore go and make disciples of all nations, baptizing them in the name of the Father and of the Son and of the Holy Spirit, and teaching them to obey everything I have commanded you" (Matt. 28:19–20).

> Proclaiming the news of Christ is not limited to simply giving out pamphlets or going door to door. It is being willing to change your barbershop, if necessary, to be a witness of the gospel of Jesus.

"Those who accepted his message were baptized. . . . They devoted themselves to the apostles' teaching and to the fellowship, to the breaking of bread and to prayer" (Acts 2:41–42).

In the movie *Men of Honor*, Master Chief Billy Sunday, a Navy diver, was asked by a young diver, "How many lives have you saved?" The master chief turned to the young diver and said that he had lost count of how many lives he'd saved, but could tell him exactly how many he had lost.

God has blessed us to see more than two hundred people come to know Christ as Lord in our first year of ministry, but as great as this is, the work of The EDGE is just beginning. We must create more opportunities for new believers to be discipled. But as with most churches and nonprofit organizations, we don't have the manpower to appoint coaches for everyone. We do, however, provide opportunities for group, special interest, and individual mentorships to take place.

Older men hang out with the youth to be examples to young men and, hopefully, begin a healthy mentoring relationship. More seasoned married couples pour into younger couples. The opportunities are many and varied.

Growth

"Therefore, I urge you, brothers [and sisters], in view of God's mercy, to offer your bodies as living sacrifices, holy and pleasing to God. . . . Do not conform any longer to the pattern of this world, but be transformed by the renewing of your mind" (Rom. 12:1–2).

Author Tom Clancy once said, "Life is about learning; when you stop learning, you die." The EDGE is all about being intentional and relevant in moving people from Similac baby formula to Gerber baby food to real meat. That is, through an intentional change in spiritual diet, individuals will begin to explore who they are in Christ and how to live according to the Spirit.

We desire disciples who become spiritual self-feeders, a process that looks different for every individual. Cypher groups (small groups) are the primary means to start this growth. These groups range in demographics with men, women, teens, and young adults.

Empowerment

"For I know the plans I have for you . . . plans to prosper you and not to harm you, plans to give you hope and a future" (Jer. 29:11).

Knowing the self-centered culture of hip-hop, we intentionally started from day one to talk about making disciples. We strongly believe that a healthy church produces people who can make disciples themselves. But we don't stop there.

We want to provide opportunities for everyone in the body of Christ and The EDGE to fulfill their calling, whether it's a young rapper or poet who needs help growing his gift, a kid from the hood who would like to go to college, or the kids we hire to work in the ministry. We feel it is the church's responsibility to introduce all in the body to hope and a future.

NOTE

1. Peter C. Wagner, *Church Planting for a Greater Harvest: A Comprehensive Guide* (Ventura, Calif.: Regal, 1990), 16.

THE CHURCH APPLIED

Every church is called to reach beyond itself.

I have lived in both urban and suburban communities; I have also been a member and leader in urban and suburban ministries. As I gained invaluable experience in both environments, I discovered one piece of common ground: We create isolated bubbles of social numbness to anything outside our immediate circles, whether we live in- or outside the city.

An inner-city church's leadership and congregation can become so preoccupied with its own brokenness and community that it doesn't reach beyond the confines of those in its pews (or chairs). I've noticed that often even large urban churches don't have an outreach pastor. While not a huge issue, it does point to the missional temperature of the church.

A well-respected inner-city leader once told me, "The black church does not have the money to pay anyone." I understand fully the pain of not having financial resources to staff a ministry as we desire. I responded to him by saying, "But our biggest asset is people who will volunteer when resources are low."

I actually don't think the lack of outreach in the urban church is due to lack of human resources. I believe that such outreach and its resulting community transformation must be a core value of the lead pastor, leadership team, and congregation as a whole.

BOTH JERUSALEM AND THE ENDS OF THE EARTH

On the other hand, suburban churchgoers want to get to the service early to get a good seat, then rush out the minute the service is over to avoid parking lot congestion (sounds to me like a trip to the movies). This fast-paced, anti-communal environment ultimately kills outreach participation. Nobody knows, has time, or really cares about opportunities.

> When the Christian church lives in isolation within their respective urban/suburban ghettos and not in relationship, it is nearly impossible to face the implications of covenant life within the church.

In our suburban gated communities and pretty cul-de-sacs, the idea of community is a foreign concept not to be explored. Thinking beyond individual households—often with their own fenced backyards—isn't even considered. Cold, nonrelational mission trips and brief service projects are a cheap substitute for building authentic relationships for the sake of the gospel.

Urban folks ask themselves: Are we really important or just a project? Are you really committed as a brother, or will your commitment wane when the true cost of urban ministry is understood? Are you as concerned about my kids as you are your own?

When the Christian church lives in isolation within their respective urban/suburban ghettos and not in relationship, it is nearly impossible to face the implications of covenant life within the church. In part, it is a lack of understanding of what it means to be in covenant with God and our brothers and sisters, but it is also as simple as out of sight, out of mind. Isolation is a form of protection against the realities faced by those different from ourselves. Without relationship and an understanding of the covenant bond between all Christians, we can easily dismiss our calling, responsibility, and ministry to those around us.

We all see the impact of poverty, drug infestation, and gangs in the urban centers in the form of skyrocketing prison populations, increased crime, failing urban schools, teen pregnancy, and inadequate healthcare. Yet many in the urban churches simply look the other way; and suburban churches jump over their cities to fly thousands of miles away to help impoverished people in other countries.

I certainly understand the need and call to help those in other countries, but I also see the need and feel the call to help those within arm's reach. Are they any less hungry, defeated, or alone?

I believe we must reassess where our Judea is. Consider how we typically read the very familiar Acts 1:8: "But you will receive power when the Holy Spirit comes on you; and you will be my witnesses in Jerusalem, *then* in all Judea and Samaria, *then* to the ends of the earth."

> We are called to reach the lost both far and near at the same time. In both the inner-city and suburban context, we must rediscover the meaning of Jerusalem and Judea.

By using the word *then*, we act as if there is some chronological order to getting the Word out and seeing about the needs of broken people. The verse actually reads: "But you will receive power when the Holy Spirit comes on you; and you will be my witnesses in Jerusalem, *and* in all Judea and Samaria, *and* to the ends of the earth" (emphasis added).

I believe the verse suggests that we are called to reach the lost both far and near at the same time. In both the inner-city and suburban contexts, we must rediscover the meaning of Jerusalem and Judea. In most churches, leaders are not training our next generation to feel the pain and brokenness of people within driving and walking distance of the church.

When was the last time someone contacted you crying about the young man selling drugs on the street corner or had a request for support because a family feels the call to pack up everything and move to the inner city?

I know that some urban and suburban ministries are doing a great job reaching the inner city. I applaud these efforts, as well as suggest that those not reaching the inner city consider how they might join the good fight.

> I've seen it happen often, though: gang leaders, pimps, and prostitutes reach out to the broken and lost more effectively and intentionally that we do in the church.

Unfortunately, the body of Christ has shown very little desire to reach the lost if it means crossing racial and economic barriers in both urban and suburban contexts. The well-known biblical story of the good Samaritan offers several nuggets of truth we can use as we reach out to the urban culture (Luke 10:25–37). For Jesus to use a Samaritan as an example of "good" was a slap in the face to the religious leaders of his day. In that day, *Samaritan* and *good* were not used in the same sentence. By doing so, Jesus suggested that who they (and we) viewed as the scum of the earth represented the principles of Scripture better than the religious folks do. The idea of a Samaritan doing more for the injured man than a priest and Levite challenged the religious system of the day.

I've seen it happen often though: gang leaders, pimps, and prostitutes reach out to the broken and lost more effectively and intentionally than we do in the church. They may have a sinful ulterior motive, but they reach out nonetheless. I'm saying that, beyond strategic goals and programs, the suburban and urban church must burn with compassion for hurting people within our reach.

The good Samaritan story pushes us to step outside our comfort zone and pour ourselves and resources into another person. We can all agree on the reality of urban decay. It is time for action. It is time for Christian men and women to focus on bringing the body of Christ into visible unity, faithful obedience, and real commitment to reaching broken lives in the urban context.

TAKE IT HOME: ACTION STEPS FOR THE CHURCH

Be the Church without Walls

Our culture is trained to think of the church in terms of a service, a building, or a program instead of the incarnational Word becoming flesh and dwelling among us. Traditional thinking limits the church to a location. But we must come to the point of seeing the church embodied in relationships, teaching, discipleship, and equipping.

These concepts extend beyond the building and straight into home fellowship, neighborhood outreach, community renewal, and meaningful service projects. The truth of the gospel can be proclaimed and lived out anywhere Christians gather together. We must gather outside the walls and be among those in the heart of the community.

Move beyond Emotional or Knowledge Extremes

Generations of urban children are introduced to the God of the Bible through emotion and pastoral dictatorships. The flashy, emotional words of dynamic, all-powerful preachers are little protection against the real enemy and leave little room for questions and searching. The youth leave the church thinking God either isn't powerful enough to help them, or doesn't care enough to answer their questions, problems, or crises.

Yet the suburban tendency to teach, teach, teach leaves many wondering what to do with real life. An ivory-tower gospel does little to heal long-buried wounds and sins; instead it directs the wounded to another class or small group. It is critical that we direct all believers — suburban and urban—directly to the cross, directly to surrendering their whole hearts to the God of the universe.

Renounce Money

Luke 16:13 says, "No [one] can serve two masters. . . . You cannot serve both God and Money." Jesus doesn't get any clearer than that; but the current focus on the principles of wealth, money management, and stewardship have overrun the principles of love, community, and service. Will our church's building, programs, and bank accounts survive when the Lord returns? Will we be rewarded for practicing sound financial strategies to ensure our future or for acts of service and mercy to the poor? How can we be people and churches of faith when all our actions lead to greater security in earthly possessions?

> The current focus on the principles of wealth, money management, and stewardship have overrun the principles of love, community, and service.

I'm not suggesting we don't have some level of savings or funds set aside to ensure the presence of the church in the community. I'm reiterating the harsh reality that if the church functions merely on the principles of wealth, we cannot expect our congregations to step out in faith.

Encourage Discussion, Honesty, Honor, and Acceptance

I know that some of the stories and topics discussed in this book may make your hair stand on end. Racism, for instance, makes people uncomfortable; so does sexual abuse, drugs, and gang violence. But it is time for the church to engage nonetheless in real discussions about real issues—race, privilege, and class, for example—without fear of reprisal.

Foster Trusting Relationships

Building authentic relationships is key to establishing and maintaining a presence in any community, but those relationships take time to build.

Get to know the people around you by moving beyond statistics, surveys, and service projects.

Consistent acts of kindness in the community build relationships, as well as help you and your church truly know those you serve. This isn't about filling your church to meet your goals; this is about being good neighbors with no strings attached.

A good question to ask is this: If our church ceased to exist, would we be missed in our community? If so, you have been effective in building relationships in the community. If not, it's time to get busy. Relationship building is essential for any church, but is especially so for urban churches.

Promote Acts of Service and Mercy

Because trust is such a major obstacle in urban ministry, the church must look for opportunities to overcome trust barriers. Many service ministries respond too slowly to the needs of the people, yet there is such a sense of urgency when someone is in need. Quick response builds trust. Think of a twenty-year-old mother with two children and no family to depend on; she's going to school and her car breaks down. She is near a breaking point with no help in sight.

> A good question to ask is this: If our church ceased to exist, would we be missed in our community?

This is exactly where the gospel makes sense: Christian people stepping into relationship to stabilize a family in need. What is money for if not serving? In times of crisis, it's all about emotional support; a sense of security, dignity, and hope; and knowing that you matter and aren't alone.

Pursue Cultural Relevance

Whether we like it or not, cultural relevance is vital. I'm not telling you to wear your hat backwards and start rapping. I am saying that churches in America have long been structured with the mono-cultural experience in mind. I'm not even saying every urban church should be converted to a hip-hop church. The responsibility of the local church, though, is to determine what is relevant in its context.

We need to think about urban ministry the same way we think about missions: we must understand the local meaning behind the way we present truth. Words such as *father*, *family*, *love*, *son*, and *hope* have different meanings in a setting where Satan and this world have created a culture of abuse, poverty, and violence.

We must be aware of a cultural bias that makes us think we must stick to best practices and methods found in the materials we read. What works in a wealthy, white, suburban church probably isn't going to work in a diverse, urban church. What works for Asian churchgoers may not work for Hispanic or black worshipers.

Every urban ministry must have an intentional plan to raise up leaders who represent and honor the community. And honestly, in the hip-hop culture this isn't easy. Many barriers to effective leadership take time to overcome, so the church must be sold on commitment to local leadership despite the many bumps in the road.

Embrace Multicultural Community

Church leaders need to understand that multicultural ministry isn't natural in the United States. By nature and formerly by law, we segregate. You might say, "I don't have any people different from me in my neighborhood." I heard a pastor respond to such a statement with, "If you can go to your local Walmart and see people of different colors, you have the possibility of people from different walks of life in your church."

One downfall of urban churches is that while urban centers are melting pots for many cultures, church demographics don't reflect this. If a church isn't intentional about creating an environment for all people, it won't happen naturally.

God has proven through The EDGE that he has no limits. People of different racial, economic, and religious backgrounds worship and fellowship in Jesus' name to the sounds of hip-hop in the background. Some have told me that they don't especially like the music, but the love, acceptance, and community keeps them coming back. A visiting Czech Republic pastor attended a session one Saturday. He reported to a friend that the music and message were awesome, but he was most impressed with the sense of community among the people.

> If a church isn't intentional about creating an environment for all people, it won't happen naturally.

Partner with Purpose

Suburban and urban churches need to ask a hard question regarding doing ministry together: Do we want a partnership or project? Projects tend to bear little long-term fruit if they lack local support because there is little investment in the lives of others. Individual and group needs are left unidentified, burdens are not shared, and people end up alone again.

A partnership with an urban church requires shared ministry goals but with a willingness to share the burdens and heavy lifting necessary to deal with the challenges of urban life. Such a partnership is long-term; it will be costly; there will be failures; it requires taking risks and demonstrating humility, patience, and grace. But the urban culture is where the battle is waged, the need is great, and the heart of God rests.

AFTERWORD

Several themes seem to undergird my life, but perhaps *undergird* is too strong a word with its connotations of strength and solidness. *Thread* might be a better descriptor. My life so often seemed to hang by a thread, even as it rested on underpinnings as fragile as threads. Let me share these threads, along with the words of my mom, Linda Love, and my wife, LaDawn Thomas-Evans, as they remember and we review the life of that boy and the man I became.

PERCEIVED ACCEPTANCE

I did not know who I was. I didn't feel as though I fit in anywhere. For as long as I can remember, I felt different. Not that my values were all bad: I worked, cooked, and babysat from about age ten, which put me in a strange place. How many eleven-year-olds can make a several-course meal, make money on a hustle of some sort, save money, and prepare a bottle of Enfamil for their siblings?

Even before I got involved in the lifestyle I chose, these things set me apart from the pack. They seem admirable from an adult perspective, but as a kid I just thought I was different.

Linda recalls:

I thought Troy was perfect. He was fun, always a dancer. He liked clothes a lot, but he didn't care about name brands. He had a lot of friends, the girls always liked him, and he got along with his sisters and brothers. But he wasn't a school person. He didn't tell me until later that one of his teachers said he'd never do anything with his life. But I just thought he was the perfect kid.

Nevertheless, it seemed that trouble always found me. Big or small things at school or home always had me on some punishment docket. As soon as I was free of a punishment (like being grounded), I'd do something else wrong and be right back in my room. After awhile, I felt like I was incapable of doing anything good, while my "perfect" brother Mark never did anything bad. And it seemed like my sister Lisa could tear up the world and get away with it.

> I was isolated often because of bad behavior; I felt unaccepted from many directions.

Though I now believe my parents were more than fair, punishments left me isolated once again. Everyone else was outside on a hot summer afternoon, but I was stuck inside serving my sentence. I pushed away even more from my family. My love language, affirmation, was not being spoken; I was isolated often because of bad behavior; I felt unaccepted from many directions.

By not wanting a relationship with me, my biological father left me struggling with a whole different level of acceptance, which I still struggle with today. Just last year he asked me to be his friend on Facebook. My hopes were high, thinking he wanted to stay in touch, to build a relationship with me. I checked my inbox every couple of days, but nothing. I went to his page to ask, "What's up?" I left a personal message. Nothing. Once again I was broken, upset, and left feeling unaccepted, a feeling that stems from that deep hole in my youthful heart.

Linda:

Troy left home, but I didn't know much of what was going on. I heard about the gang and the fighting, but he never brought any of that stuff around the house. I didn't know he was sneaking out, didn't know Mark was opening the door for him. Before Troy moved out, Gaylord told him that if he couldn't follow the rules of the house he would have to leave, but I respected Troy in that he asked me if he could leave home. I was sad, though. I didn't know why he would want to leave me.

When Mark got shot and they called me down at the Amway Grand Plaza, I thought they had made a mistake. Mark didn't hang out like that; I thought it was Troy who had been shot. With all the stuff I'm finding out now—the stuff he's telling me and testifying about in church—I feel like people are asking, "What kind of mother did he have that she didn't know all this stuff?" But I worked second shift, getting home at 11 p.m. or whenever, so Gaylord was there or I took them to my mother's.

LACKING CHRISTIAN INFLUENCE

There were always men hanging around the house or the neighborhood when I was a kid. Some were better than others, of course. My uncle sat out on the porch and got drunk most nights. Our neighbor beat his woman and was the biggest drug dealer on our side of

> I truly needed men of God to teach and guide me.

town. My cousins were just as lost as I was. The men in my birth dad's family didn't reach out to me.

Gaylord, my dad in real life, was the strongest man and greatest provider that I've ever known. But the fact remains that none of these were men of God. I truly needed men of God to teach and guide me. The kind of spiritual influences I needed were absent.

> Unfortunately, the church was unwilling to be relevant; it left me bleeding on the curb, crying for help and hope.

I am grateful for the time I spent in Sunday school, even though I was strictly there for the ladies. My heart longed for the truth of God's love to be presented in a way that made sense. I had real issues that needed to be met, and the only way to meet them was with the hope of the gospel.

Unfortunately, the church was unwilling to be relevant; it left me bleeding on the curb, crying for help and hope. I couldn't understand what the church was saying. I was eager to receive good news, but I heard only confusing words through mediums I couldn't relate to. It was easy for the church to tell me that I had to get into the Word, but I couldn't read, and the idea of trying made me frustrated and feeling like I was so dumb it wasn't worth trying.

LaDawn recalls:

We drank heavily, but one day out of the blue, I said I didn't want to drink anymore. He didn't know what was up, but I said it just smelled and tasted wrong, that I just couldn't deal with it. I also told him I wanted to go back to church. I went back that week and several other weeks. The weekend of Father's Day we had been drinking and he got sloppy drunk, which was strange for Troy to get so drunk on just one or two beers.

Sunday morning we were hearing the same message from Jesse DuPlantis about being a real man. I was weeping, but it wasn't about

Troy. It was about my own father void. That was the first day I really accepted Christ as my daddy, not just this big mean guy in the sky. I was so overwhelmed with tears as I went to the altar that I didn't see anyone. We went through the salvation steps and prayer, then I opened my eyes to return to my seat. Troy was standing right next to me. Neither of us knew the other was there. I was crying and he was crying. It was beautiful and I'll never forget it.

RITES OF PASSAGE

I never had a clear picture of what it meant to move from boyhood into manhood. My rites of passage were sex and getting paid for taking care of my business (selling drugs, cutting hair, etc.). If these were signs of manhood, I was a man at age eleven.

I didn't understand what becoming a man really meant, nor did I desire real manhood until my early twenties. Recognizing that I needed to grow up was only the beginning of the process; I didn't really take the first steps until I was nearly thirty. That meant my family and ministry had to grow up with me, growing pains and hurt feelings included.

LaDawn:

Our lives changed at the very moment of salvation. We had to ask ourselves what we were going to do because we lived in the same house. We knew sleeping together was wrong, but should I move back with my mom? We decided to sleep in separate bedrooms, but that was awful. We wanted to hurry up and get married, so we did. We had a wedding in Grand Rapids.

Initially I didn't see God's hand in our lives; I saw my hand. I wanted to fill a void; I wanted a man. If he was nice, he could come. I didn't know what God was doing. But it's scary. When I share my testimony with other ladies, I talk to them about how my life could have been totally different. You get an unsaved boyfriend, but it doesn't usually work out. My life worked out for the very best, but it also could have been the worst.

Sometimes a saved girl will get an unsaved guy and try to fix him up or think she can. But that is taking a huge chance.

Linda advises mothers:

Communication is good; talk to your kids. Even though I worked a lot, weekends were for the kids. I'm doing a lot now with my grand-kids that I wish I could have done with my children. Kids grow so fast; they're little one day and the next day they're gone.

Troy texts me all the time, saying, "I love you, Mommy." I text him back, too. One day I didn't text him back right away, so he texted me to say he wasn't going to text me anymore. He still does, though.

LaDawn adds:

I talk to younger women about that God-shaped void we all have in our lives, and how to make sure we don't fill that void with other stuff like men, food, and material things. We can't just fill that void with whatever we think might fit in it at the moment.

Linda:

Troy is my son, and he's my pastor, and he's my friend. Troy takes his daughters on date nights and he tells them that he loves them. He tells the men in the church to tell their daughters that they love them so the girls don't have to hear it from the men on the street.

LaDawn:

My life with Troy now is a fairy tale. He's always been a sweet, kind, loving, considerate person; but as the years go by it gets better. We never have sharp words. He's a great husband, awesome father, and a good role model to kids around. Troy is what he is and that's what I love about him. He's a strong, godly man, and he's covering our family in that same thing so we can all walk out with that same godly character. I thank God for Troy's leadership in our home and in the church. God must think I'm the bomb because he hooked me up!

MY CHALLENGE TO YOU

I am thankful and humbled at your willingness to have taken time to read this book. My hope is that you have been encouraged and challenged to see what your role might be in reaching the lost for Christ. But specifically, I challenge you to ask the hard question of whether you are called to be a part of what God is doing in our urban centers across the country.

As you consider where God would have you serve, here are a few ways you can become engaged: pray, go, and give.

Pray

"Therefore confess your sins to each other and pray for each other so that you may be healed. The prayer of a righteous man is powerful and effective" (James 5:16).

One part of ministry that we underutilize is the power of prayer. Ministry is challenging in so many ways. Those of us in the trenches of urban ministry are often put in harm's way as we work. I venture to say that if an urban ministry worker is not in harm's way from time to time, then that person needs to move deeper into the work. That said, I solicit the prayers of the body of Christ for all urban ministry workers in the U.S.

I ask you to pray for the safety and well-being of each one, but more importantly that we all grow deeper in love with the life-saving God of the universe. Pray not just for our own development, but that as we move among the people in generational bondage, we can operate in the power that comes only from Jesus Christ. Please pray.

Go

"After this the Lord appointed seventy-two others and sent them two by two ahead of him to every town and place where he was about to go. He told them, 'The harvest is plentiful, but the workers are few. Ask the Lord of the harvest, therefore, to send out workers into his harvest field. Go! I am sending you out like lambs among wolves'" (Luke 10:1–3).

Christians have romanticized Christ's call straight into complacency and disobedience. God has called many to get uncomfortable for the sake of the gospel, but many still sit around counting their blessings. So many sit still while a culture is dying within an hour's drive of home.

Perhaps you are a businessman who, after reading this book, knows you can reach those different from you by simply spending time and listening. Maybe you are a suburban youth worker whose job does not breathe life into you. Or you're a college student ready to take on the world, but with a different vision than when you started your education. Maybe you are an educator looking for a new set of students. Perhaps you came from the streets and your life has been changed by God. To all of you, I say go.

Give

"Each [of you] should give what he has decided in his heart to give, not reluctantly or under compulsion, for God loves a cheerful giver" (2 Cor. 9:7).

Lack of resources is a major barrier in the urban context and its communities, which spills over into the ministries working in those areas. Partnering denominations and churches often support urban churches for two or three years in the hopes that the churches will become self-sustaining. As much of a blessing as that support is for the time it lasts, support is often cut off before the ministry (and its people, for that matter) are able to stand alone.

The reality is that those of us serious about urban ministry and community development know the process will take years to accomplish. Because the spiritual and social needs of people are so great, urban churches often need more staff than our suburban counterparts. Pulling the plug on financial support too early in the fight has been a major downfall of many urban ministries.

Those of you gifted to bless others financially, no matter the amount, to you I say give.

I hope I have challenged and educated you—challenged you to consider supporting or entering ministry in an urban setting, and educated you about the hip-hop culture and urban life. But most importantly, I pray that you have drawn closer to God and to his calling on your life.

POSTSCRIPT

Gotti and I go way back. We've been enemies and best friends. We've gotten drunk together, fought side-by-side, dealt drugs, and punished gang members who crossed the line.

When the General of the gang passed away, Gotti, his nephew, stepped into the role. He was a man whose word was obeyed on the street and at home. Remember that I had to ask his permission to write this book about my gang experiences. When I asked him, he told me he'd never leave the gang because he found love and acceptance there.

As the gang leader, he commanded a group of young thugs who were eager to prove themselves to him and gain respect on the streets. For most of his life, Gotti, whose real name is John McKinney, had been involved in gangs.

We remained friends when I returned to Grand Rapids despite our very different lifestyles and beliefs. Our friendship took a unique turn several years ago when he called me at my Red Cross office.

"Bat, I believe God is working in me to make some changes, and you're the dude to help me," he said.

I was stunned. He had just been named the general of the gang, which I figured would thrill him. But I wasn't going to argue with God over his work in Gotti's life. I invited him to join me for a gang conference I hosted. The *700 Club* and the Christian Broadcasting Network covered this, putting both Gotti and me on screen. Gotti declared himself a Christian on national television, but he was a gang leader through and through.

Gotti and I connected several times in 2009 and 2010. He'd come to me with questions and needs, and I'd respond, following God's leading.

"Years ago Troy had a revelation," said Gotti. "When Troy followed God back from Atlanta, his words to me were, 'If it ain't positive, I ain't with it.' I took this as a lack of respect for me and the gang, but looking back I see those were the signs of a man being born again."

Gotti, his wife DeDe, and their kids began visiting The EDGE every once in a while. We'd talk and have a good time. I knew he was working on some things in his life. He was about thirty-five, the age at which members can retire from the gang without recrimination. I sensed that he was searching, that he was watching my life to see, perhaps, how to live outside the gang and follow Jesus.

I finished this book in mid-December 2010. Just before Christmas, The EDGE had a baptism service during which we challenged people to surrender to the Lord right then and there and immediately get baptized. This was a powerful time at The EDGE, a time when we saw Jesus work in many lives.

Jesus worked in John McKinney's life that night. One of our leaders challenged him to surrender to the Lord. This man who had hurt so many people said yes to Jesus! I had the privilege of baptizing John and DeDe that night. As I baptized this man who had seen and done terrible deeds, all I saw was a man made light by the God of Light.

"I've found a home at The EDGE," John said. "I don't have to pretend to be something I'm not. I can just be me and be comfortable with that. Troy Evans has touched my life and will continue to do so because of Christ, who dwells within him."

All I can say is that God worked in both of us. If I had not yielded to God and reached out to this known banger, I would have missed out on one of the greatest opportunities in my life so far.

John has a long road ahead of him just as I did fifteen years ago. He is learning to allow God to transform his mind into a new creature in Christ. In many ways, he is learning how to live as a civilian in a strange new world. John and I continue to talk, and I coach him in this new life. As a ministry, we are constantly looking for ways to serve John and his family to move them closer to Christ.

One of my goals for this book is to encourage readers to establish and build redemptive relationships with urban youth and those who live in the urban centers of our cities. Relationship is the most important first step. Without relationship, programs and plans come to nothing.

Gotti and I had relationship. We talked and spent time and worked through things together. I answered his questions; he felt secure enough to ask them. And God worked in a powerful way.

Seeing to the needs of the broken and lost is what we are here to do. If we aren't willing, who will be?

DISCUSSION QUESTIONS

Chapter 1

1. How open is your church to the questions of its young people? Rate its openness on a scale of one to ten. Now ask your young people the same question.
2. What mechanisms do you have in place to facilitate spiritual questions by youth and adults?
3. What curriculum do you use or have you developed to address deeper issues such as redemption and forgiveness? Spend time assessing that curriculum to ensure it is relevant.
4. What steps might you take to develop appropriate curriculum?
5. How does your church provide for the life-skills needs of your congregation?
6. How open is your church to discussions about tough issues such as sex, drugs, pornography, and violence?

Chapter 2

1. How are you encouraging cross-generational interaction within your congregation?

2. How are you encouraging the older generations to get to know the younger ones?

3. What programs might you implement to encourage such interaction?

4. What do you see as the biggest roadblocks to younger and older generations working together?

5. How do you see the different cultures within your church—youth, empty nesters, young marrieds, musicians, etc.—coming under spiritual attack? How is God using these different groups?

6. How do you define *incarnational ministry*?

Chapter 3

1. List the security measures your church uses to ensure the safety of children and youth.

2. How will the church respond to a security breach, should one occur?

3. What mechanisms do you have in place to deal with one who has experienced sexual and/or physical abuse? Do you know how to contact local law enforcement about such things?

4. How has your volunteer and paid staff been trained to recognize abuse? What steps will you take toward that training now?

5. What have you learned from dealing with such issues in the past?

6. What are the strongest and weakest areas in your church's plan to deal with abuse in the church or a child or young person who comes to you about his or her abuse?

Chapter 4

1. How do you use various forms of media in your main worship and youth services?

2. How might you encourage media literacy in your young men and women?

3. What do you have in place to address issues of self-esteem, love, and sex?

4. How are you teaching respect between the sexes, as well as appropriate masculinity and femininity?

5. To what role models are you directing your youth? How might you develop role models within the church?

6. Who and what are your youth into? Do you know what they're watching, playing, and listening to? Educate yourself now.

Chapter 5

1. How many single-parent, two-parent, and combined-family households make up your church? How are you ministering to each of these groups?

2. How many in your church are living at or below the poverty line? What does this mean for your outreach ministry and financial planning?

3. What social services do you provide, such as a food pantry, clothing closet, or life-skills training? If you do not provide these services, what information do you have available about such organizations in the area?

4. How are you working to develop male leadership in your congregation?

5. What might you provide your congregation in terms of parenting helps?

6. How are you reaching the single and newly-single members of your congregation?

Chapter 6

1. As you consider the youth and adults in your church, what foundational needs do you think might be going unmet in their lives?

2. Why do you think Maslow made physiological and security needs the base of the pyramid?

3. How does your church meet some of those foundational needs people have? How—and why—does it bypass those needs in favor of esteem and self-actualizing needs?

4. How does Jesus call us to meet people's basic needs?

5. How does the command to "love your neighbor as yourself" manifest itself in your church and its programs?

6. What are your ministry's strengths and weaknesses in meeting the needs of your congregation and community?

Chapter 7

1. What kind of mentoring strategy do you have set up in your ministry? If you don't have one, why not? If you do, how well does it work?

2. Brainstorm these three different mentoring programs and how you might implement them: peer to peer, older to younger, shared interest.

3. How are you becoming a beachhead for youth in your church and the neighborhood?

4. How have gangs influenced your youth and ministry?

5. How are individuals in your church or ministry pouring into the lives of young people? Think of concrete examples, then break down those principles into broader, church-wide experiences.

6. How can you encourage those being mentored to begin to pour into someone else?

Chapter 8

1. Describe how gang membership might mirror church membership; how gang membership might fill the need for belonging, love, and acceptance that so many youth seek.

2. Why do you think gang members pray to a higher power? Why create their own "bible" of rules, codes, and symbols?

3. Compare and contrast love, truth, peace, freedom, and justice from a gang and biblical perspective.

4. How does the freedom of Christ compare to the "freedom" of street life?

5. Why was being asked to illustrate and distribute the gang's "lit" so important to Troy? What does your answer mean for those in your ministry?

6. How do you encourage deep friendships between the youth in your church?

Chapter 9

1. Why is respect so important in street life? Is respect that important in your church? Why or why not?

2. Punishment was swift for infractions or when disrespect occurred in- or outside the gang. How do the people you know offer forms of punishment when disrespect occurs?

3. How does your church or ministry handle large and small infractions? Is there a certain sense of grudge holding, forgiveness, mercy, or rigidity?

4. How does God's offer of hope and a future compare to the gang's offer of respect, money, and fame?

5. Articulate how you would talk to a gangbanger about the differences between his or her riches and the riches God offers. Role play several scenarios.

6. How can your church or ministry offer long-term help for those wanting to leave the gang life? What mechanisms do you have in place or need to create?

Chapter 10

1. How knowledgeable are your youth about drugs? How much do you actually know about their knowledge? You may be surprised at how informed they are and how accessible drugs are.

2. How can you use a banger's inherent respect of the church to talk to him or her about God?

3. How can you connect with the gangbangers or any young people in your neighborhood? How will respect play into that connection?

4. Why is spending meaningful time with a person so important?

5. How do you define *indigenous wisdom*? How can you learn from the indigenous wisdom of the street folks, the older people, or the veterans around you?

6. How can you exhibit openness and transparency both individually and as a church or ministry?

Chapter 11

1. Does your church or ministry have a plan for reaching out to those who have spent time in prison?

2. How does your church encourage respect and kindness to those with criminal pasts?

3. What programs might you offer men and women who are trying to restart their lives? Think about mentoring, anger management, job skills, etc.

4. How comfortable are you individually and as a church dealing with those who have criminal pasts?

5. What educational opportunities might you offer? Can you connect with GED classes or offer school supplies for ex-cons and their families?

6. How might you move from offering physical to spiritual help to those in need?

Chapter 12

1. Why is commitment so important to gangs? How can the church use that emphasis to begin to minister to bangers?

2. Why is building relationship so important to working with gangs and bangers? Also, do you have a relationship with local law enforcement to help you stay aware of gang activity and symbols in your area?

3. How can your church or ministry begin encouraging parents as they fight to keep their kids out of gangs?

4. What can your church do to offer kids a safe place to hang out to lessen the temptation to hang with bangers?

5. How are you monitoring your children's social networking, friends, and media exposure?

6. How can the church and parents begin modeling a healthy work ethic, the importance of education, and authentic Christianity?

Chapter 13

1. How might you or your church be exhibiting racism? Study your language, symbols, rituals, and assumptions.

2. What mechanisms do you have in place to teach youth about other religions in order to answer their questions and inform them about the dangers?

3. How does your ministry build hope for a different and better future than that offered on the streets and in the gangs?

4. Describe your investment in the lives of those immersed in the street life.

5. What invitations are you offering those on the streets as well as those in your church who are interested in working with the urban population?

6. Describe how you might implement the invest and invite model in your ministry.

Chapter 14

1. What knowledge do you have of PTSD? If little or none, where might you gain the knowledge? More importantly, why is it important?

2. What programs does your church offer to those suffering from PTSD?

3. If you are considering a PTSD outreach program, what are your strongest assets?

4. How is a relationship with mental health professionals both beneficial and necessary?

5. How is building relationships important in the treatment of PTSD?

Chapter 15

1. How can you create a congregation of believers dedicated to winning people to Christ?

2. What learning tools do you have in place to teach youth and adults how to lead others to Christ?

3. Why is it important that all people, not just the pastors, know it's their job to help lead people to Christ?

4. Compare and contrast Saul, the great persecutor of early believers, with a gangbanger.

5. Compare and contrast Ananias, sent to pour into Saul's life, with yourself and the other believers in your church or ministry. Is it a favorable comparison?

6. Create a list of questions that can open a conversation about Jesus. Practice on each other.

Chapter 16

1. Why is church involvement so important to new believers?

2. How does your church or ministry nourish new believers? What can you do better?

3. What opportunities do you offer believers to pour into the community? What about new believers who are so often eager to make a difference in a world they once helped destroy?

4. How have you created or partnered with organizations or ministries that help former bangers or criminals begin leading productive lives? Why?

5. Why is service to others vital to all believers?

6. Why is maintaining dignity important in helping new believers rebuild their lives?

Chapter 17

1. Why is forgiveness important in the life of a believer, but vital to those coming out of the street life?

2. How does our justice system as well as racism and fear hinder starting over for those who want to?

3. How might your church unknowingly further white privilege when it comes to education, housing, health care, employment, and so on? How could your church address these issues?

4. How has your church or ministry educated its people on issues of racism?

5. Examine your policies, beliefs, and practices in light of social, economical, racial, and ethnic prejudices. Where are you falling short? Where are you unwittingly hurting those in your congregation?

6. How do you respond to Troy's expressive essay?

Chapter 18

1. Has your church considered a church plant? Why or why not? What were the greatest obstacles?

2. Take a hard look at your church's target audience, location, and typical member. Do they mesh? In other words, are you an urban church with suburban members? Are you reaching into the community with a message they understand?

3. Where does your church get its new members? What does this say about your missional spirit, the unspoken messages to those who walk in the door, and your goals and policies?

4. Describe and dissect the mission and vision of your church or ministry. What do those statements say about your church? Do they contrast with actual practice?

5. What does The EDGE mean by "environment"? What is the environment in your church? What is meant by organic and strategic?

6. How does your church work out the call to evangelism, discipleship, growth, and empowerment?

Chapter 19

1. How has your church—urban or suburban—created an isolation bubble that prevents you from reaching beyond your immediate circle? How and why did this happen? Or, how have you kept it from happening?

2. How do you facilitate outreach and involvement outside the church doors? How do you let people know about opportunities?

3. Describe the ideal "covenant life" within the church as it relates to day-to-day living. Research Scripture if necessary.

4. How does Acts 1:8 speak into your outreach and missional policies and plans for your church?

5. How have modern principles of wealth invaded your church? How have issues such as money management and stewardship dampened your spirit for acts of service and mercy?

6. How multicultural is your church? How might you develop a more multicultural mind-set through church plants, education, and outreach?

Chapter 20

1. How can the church help parents who must work to provide for their family at the expense of time spent with their children?

2. Why is acceptance so vital to a young person? How can we facilitate that?

3. How can we build strong male role models for the young men and women in the church? How can we help fill their father voids?

4. How can we make the gospel message relevant to the urban culture without diluting or changing it?

5. How is your church reaching out with the message of Truth to the specific groups within your church: young girls and boys, teens, veterans, single moms, the elderly, former addicts, and former bangers?